More
Words
From
The Brother
Poetry that Matters

Poems by The Brother

Cover Art by Tom Landrum
Cover Design by Tom Hunter

This book is dedicated to everyone who ever took the time to plant a seed in a wretch like me and to all of those who work and walk along side of me each day.

Thank You

Beloved,

Ask James and he will tell you he is merely the one holding the pen. These words are a gift from the Holy Spirit to the Body of Christ that is why James has chosen to use "The Brother" as his pen name because it is not about James it is all about Jesus!

May these simple words ever serve as a reminder of the unquenchable love which our Lord and Saviour Jesus Christ has for each and every one of us!

Agape James

"ABBA"

The first time Your Name in Scripture is seen
In English is God in Hebrew Elohiym
It's plural in nature like three parts in One
Naming You and Your Spirit and also Your Son
Then the Lord God is what we hear next
Jehovah, I AM, the One Who protects
We hear Most High God also called El Elyon
Owner of all in the world and beyond
Next Adonai which means Husband or Master
All those who obey You will keep from disaster
Then Almighty God El Shaddai in Hebrew
To be perfect You tell us to walk before You
Everlasting God also called El Olam
In Beer-Sheba this Name came from Abraham
Jehovah Jireh the next Name we hear
God will provide my son have no fear
Then You said to Moses I AM that I AM
The unchanging God who led Abraham
You also said from sickness You'd free
You said I AM the Lord that healeth thee
The Lord is my Banner is what is proclaimed
When Jehovah Nissi is the Name that is named
Jehovah Shalom simply means You are Peace
Forever and ever may this Name never cease
Lord of Sabaoth also called Lord of Hosts
Of minions and armies You have the most
Jah is a short Name but strong in it's form
Like thunder that rolls and rumbles a storm
These are a few of the Names You have used
And so many more when Your heel it was bruised
But we call You Father or ABBA the One
When we pray to You in the Name of Your Son

"A Boy's Life"

Preserve me O God in Thee do I trust
As I tread on this sod purge my heart of all lust
My soul cries to Thee my Lord and my Master
In You I am free on my own is disaster
The Saints You have sent on the earth have shown me
How a life should be spent that it may glorify Thee
The things they've endured all the pain and the sorrow
It's Your Word they've secured so we have it tomorrow
When I think of their pain their fate and their plight
Like Your cool latter rain in their joy I delight
But those who chase idols and serve a false god
Shall never find joy for their thinking is flawed
Lord You are my Portion and the Gift of my cup
I look not to the world for You fill me up
The lines You have drawn on the earth for my feet
Guide me each day on Your path I'm complete
You've given me counsel You teach me at night
Your knowledge is sound Your wisdom is right
You're always before me always at my right hand
You never ignore me in You I will stand
My heart is made glad my hope is Your glory
For You are my Dad and I'm in Your story
You left not my soul deep down in hell
I won't rot in that hole You've broken that spell
You've shown me the path of life in Your presence
Forever partaking of Your holy essence
Fill me up Lord in the fullness of joy
For You are my Dad and I am Your boy
(Lamentations 3:24-26)

"Acceptance"

Considering conditions and how to make it through
Please remind me first to pray and always look to You
Though fraught with many perils this long and narrow trail
With You who goes before me I simply will not fail
Balance and discernment two vital things I need
Patience and acceptance to go just where You lead
Teach me that not all things yes even when they're good
May be Your will for my life yet prompt me when I should
Just take a step of faith out to walk upon the waves
And help to spread the message that only Jesus saves
Let all my earthly passions be given up to You
That I might live the victor's life that You would have me to
Let all my actions honor Your Name in every way
A shining bright example that points to You each day
I yearn to be the man that Your Word bids me be
Fully trusting In You that all may simply see
Miraculous amazing refreshed and oh so new
Transformation unsurpassed by anything but You
Submitting to the ones whom You have placed above
A picture of your passion and only done through love
Please give me now the patience the hunger and the thirst
For genuine sincerity to always put You first
The path before me lightened that I may see the way
And be Your willing servant each and every day
My heart is full to bursting all I ever want to do
With joy that comes from serving and only comes from You

"Addiction"

You think you're tough you think you're cool
I'll take your sorry butt to school
You think you're bad you think you're mean
I'll show you things you've never seen
You think you're smooth you think you're slick
But I'll use every dirty trick
You think you'll try me just one time
I'll turn you to a life of crime
Now you might think you've got the knack
But I will straight up break your back
I'll take your kids your job your wife
And I will devastate your life
Now you might think there's nothing left
But I'm unstoppable at theft
I'll take your teeth I'll rot your skin
You'll be a slave to your own sin
I'll take your freedom and your breath
And when I'm done I'll bring you death
Now you might think that you can touch
My friend I think you think too much
I am addiction I am for real
You best think twice and that's the deal

"A Devil's Hell"

Hearken my friend and I will tell
What to expect if you go to hell
First you'll be judged and the glory you'll see
Will be in your mind for eternity
The beauty the love and the peace you've forsaken
The first pang of hell is that you were mistaken
Condemned and cast out and sent on your way
For you owe a debt and there's hell to pay
Evil you'll sense and great fear and terror
As despair racks your soul at the thought of your error
The heat is extreme and foul is the stench
The pain of each breath cause your guts to wrench
Tormentors will greet you with fetters and chains
Where the worm dieth not and there's no end to pains
No water no air no sleep no relief
No escape from your doom no end to your grief
Unquenchable thirst and sorrows untold
As your mind contemplates how your fate will unfold
The screams that you hear are solely your own
And they fall on no ears for you are alone
Before it's too late you should quit playing games
For there'll be no escape from that great lake of flames
Don't turn down God's gift don't follow the liar
Don't trade paradise for an endless hell fire

"A Father's Heart"

A father's heart cannot be tamed

When broken though it's sorely maimed

The pain and anguish that he knows

Are stretching him and so he grows

A father's heart is full of hope

His faith and love they help him cope

No matter what he has no doubt

That everything will be worked out

A father's heart is tender true

Touched with all that he goes through

And though it's tender it is strong

It needs to be to suffer long

A father's heart will find a way

To show the things he has to say

And when his love is truly shown

A father's heart is fully known

"Amazing Grace"

The cattle on a thousand hills
The waterfalls the rocks the rills
The amber waves of summer grain
That owe their strength to gentle rain
The power of a thunderstorm
The anger in a hornet's swarm
The endless reach of outer space
The smile on a child's face
A brother's strong and steady hand
That helps you when it's hard to stand
The tall majestic redwood tree
The billows tossed upon the sea
The single tender growing shoot
That grows into a tree with fruit
The birds that shuttle on the wing
The joy they trumpet when they sing
A piercing chill a winter wind
The truth of knowing I have sinned
A cool caress a summer breeze
Your mercy when I'm on my knees
In all these things I see Your face
Reflecting Your amazing grace

"Amazing Love"

A greater love doth not exist
Than that which comes from God
For He was sent to intervene
And heal that which was flawed
Unmatched in His mercy
This God which I now serve
How precious is His gift of life
Though death's what I deserve
Exquisite in its magnitude
No way to ever measure
The endless reach of outer space
Nor God's eternal treasure
No romance no friendship and no family tie
Could ever compare
To The Love that won't die
The Way of Agape
'Tis selfless and pure
He loves me regardless
Of that I am sure
His love for me is endless
He plays no silly games
So I will cry until I die
His Name above all names

"Arise"

Awake thou that sleepest
Arise from the dead
Christ shall give thee light
With it ye shall be led

Arise Arise
And open up your eyes
And you shall have the Truth
To battle Satan's lies

See then that ye walk
That straight and narrow line
Stand upon the Rock
And you will be just fine

Redeem the time
Make your days worthwhile
Live your life for Him
And He will make you smile

So be ye not unwise
And be not drunk with wine
But fill yourself with Him
And stay upon the Vine

"Armour On"

The night is far spent the day is at hand
Come now Lord Jesus teach me to stand
Strengthen me Lord in the power of Your might
And teach me to don Your armour of light
For though I am flesh I war not within it
The battle goes on and I need to be in it
My weapons aren't carnal but mighty through You
For tearing down strongholds and rebuilding them true
For casting down lies and every high thing
Take my thoughts captive and let Your truth ring
I need Your whole armour for the wiles of the devil
As he's raising his standard to a whole 'nother level
For it's not flesh and blood but dark rulers and powers
And evil magicians in white ivory towers
They lie to our daughters and they lie to our sons
But they've yet to encounter Your true holy ones
Give to me now Your armour of light
Formed from Your wisdom to fit me just right
Stand me up Lord with my loins girt about
Your truth in my bowels with not one single doubt
Please plate my breast with brilliant white light
Fill my heart Father with all that is right
Let my feet now be shod in truth let them be cleated
With Your flowing Gospel from on high where You're seated

Above all these things in faith let me be shielded
My trust in You quenching all the darts they have wielded
Encircle my brow with Your helm of salvation
Shine light on my path as I walk through creation
Teach me to wield the Sword of the Spirit
The brethren will know the truth when they hear it
It's quick and it's strong and it's sharp as a razor
Never missing the mark as precise as a laser
With prayers from the saints due diligence done
Offered up in the Spirit to Father and Son
Give to me Father a tongue that is bold
Your Word flowing freely more precious than gold
Teach me to speak Your truth in pure love
Led by Your Spirit from on high up above
Leading my brothers through the dark night
Forsaking all others bathed in Your light
Committed only to You our one Lord and Saviour
Each one tried and true and refusing to waiver
Lead us we plead by Your rod and your staff
Keep us Your seed while discarding the chaff
Restore us revive us make us Your own
Set our foundation firmly on Stone
We thank You our Father for all You have done
But mostly we thank You for sending Your Son!
(Romans 13:12, 2 Corinthians 10:3-6, Ephesians 6:10-20)

"Assurance"

It's hard to watch the ones you love
Not depend on God above
To see them struggle through this life
Fraught with worry stress and strife
The constant creep of fear and doubt
The drain of trying to think it out
And worse than all I've so far penned
No assurance for their end
A heart of fear and unbelief
Compounds a family's heartfelt grief
But oh the inner peace we get
When we know they are well met
And so I say it is a crime
To not share Christ while there's still time
To speak the truth in humble love
To pray for guidance from above
A burden has been placed on me
Please Father let my Dad now see
Your Way Your Truth Your Life Your Son
Before his time on earth is done
I pray for strength and courage to
Share with him the gift of You

"Authority"

Author – It – He
He's the One who sets us free
He's the One who hung the stars
He's the One who heals our scars
His heel it crushed the serpent's head
Our Father raised Him from the dead
He raised the mountains poured the seas
Formed the flowers and the trees
He lights the day and sends the wind
He washes clean all those who've sinned
He gives us sight to see Him true
But only those who ask Him to
He commands angelic hosts
We hear Him through His Holy Ghost
He sovereign that means He rules
The Saints His servants the wicked His tools
No thing takes place without His nod
He's in control for He is God
He wrote it all for us to see
That's why we call it His-story

"B.O.W."
(Bread On Water)

For the sake of my wife my sons and my daughters

I'm casting my bread out on the waters

Our family is broken completely in shambles

With me in the joint and them out in the brambles

But I cannot save them I have to fix me

Or else I am useless that is the key

I've sent off a letter to Standing Stones

There's nourishment there to strengthen my bones

My hands on the plow no looking back

God has my kids they'll have no lack

He covered them then He'll cover them now

Till He's satisfied that I have learned how

Thank You Lord God that You've filled my heart

With the hunger to serve and just do my part

"Babygirl"

Babygirl I love you so
There are some things you need to know
It's not fair that I'm not there
But never think that I don't care
You are my precious Babygirl
You are my heart you are my world
It's not your fault that I am here
I've made mistakes it's my fault dear
I got in trouble I was bad
But honey I am still your Dad
And though we are so far apart
I carry you within my heart
Through every moment and each mile
One thought of you just makes me smile
And though I can't see you today
Very soon we'll run and play
I promise you when I get out
We'll have our time so have no doubt
You are God's gift my precious pearl
You are my jewel my Babygirl!!!

Love Daddy

"Backup"

The Lord is my light and my salvation

In Him I will fight the decay of my nation

He is my strength my eyes He's made clear

With Him in my life whom shall I fear

When oppressed by the wicked and dogged by my foes

He has my back while increasing their woes

Though many may gather and against me they rise

I shall not retreat nor make compromise

One thing I've desired with my whole heart

To dwell in His house and never depart

For in time of trouble the gate He will lock

And stand me up firmly upon His Rock

In victory and glory my head He will raise

As I sing forth His praises for all of my days

(2 Samuel 22)

"Betrothed"

Built to go the distance locked and stocked for good
When every single instance feels just as though it should
Most precious gift from heaven her heart which is so pure
Her love for me is absolute I've never been so sure
Fifty years of aching pain and forlorn loneliness
Vanished in an instant the moment she said yes
I cherish now the heartache the doubt the fear the pain
Forgiven sinner's gratitude for sin's bright crimson stain
O dry and barren landscape so long my hearts abode
No end in sight my fearful plight while on that dusty road
Then one day like a whirlwind she came blowing in
Scattering the fallen leaves and ashes from my sin
Now standing in the garden before Your tree of life
My heart no longer hardened as I gaze upon my wife
Sweetest smelling savour blowing through the leaves
Your blossoms fragrant essence born aloft upon the breeze
Peaceful in the shade here my shelter from the storm
No longer cold and lonely but calm and safe and warm
And though the fruit looks tempting and fully ripe to pick
The thought of causing her to sin it simply makes me sick
Your perfect time is coming though soon it's not here yet
I will not even gamble I just won't make that bet
This tender heart You've given refreshed anew to me
My hopes and dreams now realized beyond what I could see
I love You ABBA Father You've crushed my selfish fears
You've filled my heart to bursting and wiped away my tears
Mere words don't do it justice Lord the remainder of my life
I will spend showing gratitude Your daughter now my wife
I trust You more than ever Lord I praise You for the pain
To truly cherish sunshine we must thank You for the rain
I thank you ABBA Father for courage faith and strength
Our hearts now tuned to Your will and set to go the length
Bless us more than ever fill our hearts with boundless joy
With full run of the garden as Your shining girl and boy!

(Proverbs 13:12)

"Bound"

Grateful for Your mercy Your love Your peace Your grace
And for Your light and warmth that gently bathes my face
For when I look to You I know that everything is well
My soul's been reconciled I'm no longer bound to hell
I know that in my spirit and so I do believe
That You are always with me and that You'll never leave
I'm finding ways to worship in everything I do
And giving all the glory back wholly unto You
I never want to grieve You that is not my intent
I pray my days are focused and with You they are spent
I need You every second every minute every hour
I long to walk in victory in Your redeeming power
I know that through obedience Your strength in me will grow
Your joy the fruitful harvest for godly seeds I sow
Please help me fight temptation please help me Lord to stand
A grateful willing servant Your souldier to command
I'm honored that You called me and taught me Your Son's Name
Please give me strength to never ever bring it any shame
And that with which I struggle please help me to see clear
Your will to overcome myself that I may always hear
Your still small quiet whisper that echoes in my heart
And from Your holy presence please let me not depart
I need You to remind me each and every day
For left to my devices I simply drift away
And so in desperation I cry this heartfelt plea
Lord please do not relinquish this grip You have on me

"Break Bread"

Basic Instructions Before Leaving Earth
A plan for your life before your own birth
It's not a rule book that thinking is flawed
Truly it is a love letter from God
And when you look within God's Word
Your heart will know what it has heard
Confirmation for your soul
To strengthen you and make you whole
From prophecies yet to unfold
To proverbs which ring solid gold
Precious words you will find there
Of mercy kindness love and care
Also warnings not to tread
The crooked path that leaves you dead
His Word is solid straight and true
It's how our Father talks to you
It will not change it will not break
He bids you now to come partake
The light it shines is always fresh
For it is Christ it is His flesh
The fiend was sorely stunned when smitten
As Jesus told him "It is written"
Do not forsake to learn your sword
This awesome gift straight from the Lord
Claim His promise end your strife
Come now break the Bread of Life

"Breeze Brothers"

The warm summer breeze
That caresses my face
And puts me at ease
In spite of this place
A hawk rides the wind
Outside the fence
To him the whole world
Makes perfect sense
He's shopping for dinner
I'm doing my time
I was born as a sinner
He knows nothing of crime
We both have a purpose
A place in God's plan
He soars as a raptor
I walk as a man
The same breeze he rides
Blows through my hair
Reminding us both
The Father is there

"Brotherhood"

There is someone you call first

When things are at their very worst

No matter what when things go wrong

They stand with you and make you strong

Yeah they will always have your back

And when you slip they cut you slack

Regardless of the mess you make

The bond you have it will not break

Some are blood and some are not

And sometimes they are all you've got

They are a gift with which we're blessed

And when they're real they are the best

They are there when there is no other

There's no compare to a real true Brother

"Burdened"

Burdened for the broken burdened for the lost
Prayer for them to trust the One who paid the bloody cost
So hard to watch them struggle with all they're going through
Rock bottom's what they need to find that they may cry to You
My prayer is that you give them truly open eyes
To see past the deception and the multitude of lies
Lies straight from the devil and this sin cursed broken place
And lies they tell when looking in the mirror at their own face
Regardless of the reason anger pain or simply grief
Truth or lies we feed ourselves weave the fabric of belief
There is power in believing whether wrong or truly right
Yet Truth as its revealed always brings one to the light
I pray for understanding and the courage to speak out
The truth in love with confidence and not one single doubt
But most of all I pray my Lord that you would intervene
As You did with me and You know just what I mean
My hope is they will make it safely to that restful place
Where willingly they ask and so receive Your gift of grace
I have to trust the process knowing You will work it out
As You did for me and never ever let me doubt
For this I know if you could save a broken wretch like me
You have the awesome power to set any sinner free
Let them know the only thing that truly heals comes from above
That which you give freely Your gift of pure agape love

"Changes"

Changes are coming for me and for you

Deep down in your heart you know this is true

A tree that won't bend gets snapped in the wind

And hard is the heart that says I've never sinned

The things in our pasts we've learned to endure

They've taught us to walk with a spirit that's sure

The things we can't change well those things change us

And when we accept that it is a plus

Character comes from the changes we make

And God gives us grace for the ones we can't take

Changes are vital and through them we grow

God's teaching us things in the changes we know

A sapling springs up and gets longer and longer

With each day of change it grows stronger and stronger

So don't fear the changes that come on life's path

They add to the sum of God's sovereign math

"Chin Up"

Caught up in the moment
And trying just to cope
As faith rests on the premise
That one must have some hope
The devil will distract you
And try to beat you down
He even pierced my Saviour's brow
Accursed thorny crown
But deep inside I must abide
I really need to know
That God is always with me
No matter where I go
Atop the highest mountain
Or darkest valley floor
The coolest crystal spring
Or distant bloody shore
This tiny speck we live on
Mere dust in outer space
All of this will fade away
When gazing on His face
For now just count your blessings
Yes name them one by one
And thank the Father every day
For sending us His Son

"Choose"

Wrapped up in a mystery this puzzle we call life
Enigmatic purpose fraught with pain and strife
Many search for answers reaching far and wide
When actually the key to life is buried deep inside
Love is the only reason we think and move and breathe
Love bestowed upon us that which we all receive
The righteous and the wicked the mighty and the small
For does not rain and sunshine beat down upon us all
Perception sets the attitude you're grateful or you're not
The counting of one's blessings the grateful heart is taught
The key to life above the strife the path to love and peace
Is simply trusting in the One who's promised us release
Release from all our burdens our woes our hurts our pain
For by His blood's redeeming flood
He's washed clean every stain
Now you can choose to listen or you can go your way
I promise this to you my friend that there will come a day
A day when all that matters is the truth and what you do
Receive God's gift of grace or not it's wholly up to you
For each of us is given in our hearts and minds the choice
The freedom to deny it or to listen to God's voice
The thief wants to deceive you and convince you it's a lie
But really he's the liar and he wants to see you die
Tomorrow is not promised don't put off another day
Claim the gift He offers you Christ is the only way!

"Chosen"

While walking one day by the sea on the beach

Our Lord saw two brothers He knew He could teach

He called them and told them to lay down their nets

He'd bought them to mold them and pay off their debts

Simon called Peter and Andrew his brother

They'd leave all behind and follow no other

He saw John and James with their dad Zebedee

He called out their names saying come follow Me

His plan was to guide them and teach them and then

Give them commissions as fishers of men

One day He saw Matthew counting some coin

Without looking back he was eager to join

That night at his house they had a great dinner

While vipers and scribes said He eats with a sinner

Then Thomas and Philip and Bartholomew

James son of Alpheus and Thaddeus too

Simon the zealot and Judas the traitor

Each chosen to realize their destiny later

For three years they followed wherever He went

Then after His death to the world were they sent

To carry the Gospel throughout the known lands

To set free the captives and heal with their hands

Forsaking their lives to pick up His cross

The things of this world they counted as loss

To sew up the breach the traitor had rent

They gave forth their lots and Matthias was sent

The Gospel of course was meant to save all

For this very purpose Christ picked out Saul

On the road to Damascus He blinded his eyes

He told him to wake up and quit spreading lies

He sent him on journeys of thousands of miles

To carry the Gospel to all the Gentiles

This is the story of servants and sons

Christ's holy apostles and God's chosen ones

"Clean Bill of Health"

A study in stupidity
That life that I was livin'
But oh the joy that I now know
Since I have been forgiven
Now I might not have everything
But all my needs are met
And all that will be added too
It just ain't happened yet
Seeing things for what they are
And knowing who He is
The joy and peace of knowing
Forever I am His
Beyond my comprehension
A calm envelops me
My spirit knows assurance
His peace has set me free
So what's the final finding
I've found eternal wealth
The Great Physician's Blood gives me
The cleanest bill of health

"Climb"

High atop the mountains
Where snowflakes gently land
A man can really lose himself
And come to understand
A struggle just to reach it
And though it's very cold
'Tis priceless beyond measure
Such beauty to behold
His strength and his endurance
Are put right to the test
Relentlessly ascending
On top he will then rest
A place without distractions
Just mountain, man, and God
Frosty barren mountain tops
Laid out to view unflawed
Far above the valleys deep
Strife ridden full of toil
The majesty of God's design
Transcends the mortal coil
There simply is no photo
No canvas, song, or book
That comes close to the beauty
God shows you in one look
So widen your horizons
Invest a little time
Lift your eyes up to the skies
And climb my brother climb

"Combat"

This world is cursed with sin and pollution

Don't focus on that but on the Solution

We were not designed to shout at the dark

For when we do that we're missing the mark

We can't beat the devil it's not our fight

He can only be vanquished with God's awesome might

The world and it's ways are riddled with cancer

But Christ is the Way yes He is the Answer

Don't look at the waves that crash all around

But stand on the Rock and you will not drown

For He is our Armour and He is our Shield

And His Word is the Sword He'll teach us to wield

Remember this though when wielding His Sword

The battles not ours it belongs to the Lord

So walk in His ways and always take care

And never forget the power of prayer

Don't trip on this world with its wounds and its scars

But look to the Lord and know victory's ours

"Come On"

Take His yoke upon your shoulders
Lay your cross against your back
Bind His Word upon your heart
And my friend you'll have no lack
For my Lord He will go with you
He'll not leave you nor forsake
No He'll be right there beside you
With every step you take
Leave this world behind you
Seek His kingdom first
Even when they bind you
And do their very worst
Now the devil he may trip you
But Brother get back up
For we must all be ready
When Christ calls on us to sup
With nothing we were brought here
And with nothing we shall go
But nothing here compares
To the riches we shall know
Today our Lord is calling
This is not some silly game
Don't take the chance of falling
Just call upon His Name
(Mark 8:34-38)

"CornerStone"

The Stone which the builders disallowed

Blinded they were for they were too proud

Stiff-necked and callous and full of vane pride

So set in their ways they cast Him aside

A great Stone of stone of stumbling a Rock of offense

The Way and the Truth and the Life that makes sense

The Light that's come in and shines in the dark

And gives us the power to not miss the mark

The love that He's shown the price that He paid

No other foundation than Christ can be laid

So let us transform to His image unflawed

And each stand as stones in the household of God

"Courage"

Courage looks fear straight in the eye
Courage goes on even though I may die
Deep down inside in my own secret space
It springs from the knowledge that I'm saved by grace
Courage has faith even when shaken
Courage can say yes I was mistaken
Have courage fear not God's Word has told us
For no matter what the Father will hold us
No man is able to pluck from His hand
And faith in that fact helps us to stand
Courage goes on despite our worst fears
It bears all and continues even in tears
Courage is something that God has put in us
We need it to tell folks that He came to win us
So be not afraid and look to the Lord
He's already paid so pick up His Sword
It means to take heart to stand for what's right
Firm with resolve in the power of God's might
Yes courage means heart it is what it is
And never forget that the battle is His
One final thing that I'd like to make clear
If God has my back whom then shall I fear?

(Deuteronomy 31:6)

"Creation to Cross"

O Lord our God how perfect Thy Name
Throughout all the earth and the heavens the same
You've set up Your glory high over the vault
How perfect Your story without any fault
From mouths of babes and sucklings alike
Your hammer of truth heart's anvil doth strike
Thine enemies flee with their hosts rent asunder
A whisper from You comes rolling like thunder
When I consider the works of Thine hands
The moon and the starts and the far distant lands
What is a man that Thou are mindful of him
He's weak and he's broken and riddled with sin
For his sake You've lowered Your Son to the nations
Where He walked among us with no reputation
And after He'd taught us and gave us our roles
We beat Him and scourged Him and pierced Him with holes
He took upon Him our sins and our doom
Then we laid His body deep down in that tomb
But you came and raised Him and rolled back that stone
And took Him to heaven and gave Him a throne
You crowned Him with power and honor and glory
And sent forth apostles to tell us His story
We thank You our Father for making a way
To follow Him home where forever we'll stay

(Psalm 8)

"Crossroad"

There is a road it's long and it's tough
When you are on it things may get rough
The way it is narrow and straight is the gate
There's still time to get on it before it's too late
The choice we must make to win or to lose
One way or another we all have to choose
Yeah sooner or later you gotta get right
Pull your head out and walk in the light
People will scorn you and say you're a fool
If they cause you to stumble man that ain't cool
Don't listen to them but walk with the Brothers
Concern not yourself with the approval of others
But all that you do must be done out of love
In the Name of the Father and the Son up above
Whatever you've thought you've read or you've heard
Make sure that it all lines up with the Word
There is a small voice be still and you'll hear it
Yes God speaks to us through His Holy Spirit
The world calls us fools they don't know why we bother
But we seek the Son that we might know the Father
Yes the way of the world is too much to afford
So before it's too late call on the Lord!!!

(Romans 10:13)

"Crosswalk"

Down on the corner of Thirst and Pain

Where your soul's so parched its got ya beggin for rain

When your heart's so weary and your mind's so numb

It's the call of the Master who bids you come

Now Easy street seems so wide and broad

But that's a fast-lane running away from God

And the big bright lights of Broadway call

But the higher you climb the farther you fall

And it makes no difference just who you know

There's lots of high rollers dying down on skid row

Yeah the world says man you gotta live this way

But if you don't trust Christ there's hell to pay

So bring to the Master your hopes and fears

He'll calm your storms and wipe your tears

Ask Jesus to be your First and Main

He'll meet you on the corner of Thirst and Pain

(Matthew 11:29-30)

"Crowns"

A crown of rejoicing is what we look toward
To bask in Christ's presence O what a reward
Most men seek a crown that will fade away
But ours has no end it's perfect that way
A righteous one's laid up high in that place
For all of His Saints who do love His face
Blessed is he that endureth when tempted
With life he is crowned from death he's exempted
Those feeding His sheep and telling His story
The Shepherd Himself brings them one of glory
He's promised those faithful unto the death
A sweet crown of life and endless sweet breath
A symbol of triumph in this contest of life
A token of honor for surviving the strife
But know this my brethren the whole reason why
We shall see crowns because Christ came to die
They mocked Him and beat Him and heaped on Him scorn
They made Him a crown completely of thorn
The Blood that flowed down from His head so divine
Washes us clean for it is God's wine
But I wait for the day which John has foretold
When Christ comes on a cloud crowned with pure gold

"Daily Bread"

Your attributes are plain to see

Your love Your strength Your majesty

Your mercy and Your patience too

As I fall daily short of You

For filthy are the rags I bear

Regardless still You always care

Your truths from ancient days were told

And constantly they yet unfold

You've done so much and still You give

In You we find the strength to live

And though Your love envelops me

With blessings flowing endlessly

Description truly is defied

This pen my Lord has tried and tried

Yet still You shine Your brilliant light

And so I lift this pen and write

I thank You Lord for all You've said

Yes thank You for our Daily Bread

"Darkly"

Mirror mirror on the wall
So dark it's hard to see at all
For though I'm blessed with eyes to see
The hardest thing to see is me
I long to live a simple life
A house a job a loving wife
I strive to be a simple man
But God may have another plan
Something more than nine to five
Likely why I'm still alive
Despite the mess I'd made of me
Christ's sacrifice has set me free
Free to live and laugh and love
And set my mind on what's above
To go and serve and use my voice
Reminding all they have a choice
A choice that each of us must make
When choosing though make no mistake
There's only one way whence we came
All others lead to endless flame
I long to know as I am known
And reap the harvest God has sown

"Day Planner"

The view is true from forty-two

Clearer than what I thought I knew

The stuff I did when I was just a kid

It sent my life into a fatal skid

But now I've grown and these are things I own

To stand a man a part of God's own plan

I've seen I've heard I have God's written Word

I know remorse for my misguided course

I've changed my ways and now He leads my days

My past was grim but now I follow Him

From lost to found He's turned my life around

I have received I am no more deceived

Day by day Christ lights up my way

Now this I know no matter where I go

He'll be with me when I turn forty-three

"Dayspring"

The mist that hugs the mountain peaks
The tears that stain my wind chilled cheeks
The haze that fills the slate gray sky
Another pre-spring day goes by
Dead leaves scattered on the ground
Their rustling makes a brittle sound
With echoes from an autumn past
But spring is here and that won't last
Already birds are on the wing
They flit and fly and chirp and sing
The trees are dark and gray and bare
They're barren yet no leaves are there
And though the ground has ceased to freeze
Still there is a chilly breeze
But soon the springtime will return
There's something here for us to learn
Nothing stays the same forever
Including God's sublime endeavor
The sun is followed by the moon
And Christ's return is coming soon
And though this winter's been so long
This earth will sing a brand new song
Things will change that is the way
He's one step closer every day
"Maranatha"

"Defined"

An Iron Saint is meant to be

One who sets the captives free

Sworn to serve the sovereign Lord

And versed to wield His holy sword

Igniting passions in those ones

Whom God has chosen as His sons

Speaking truth no matter what

The Gospel bold and pure uncut

For he is not ashamed to speak

He stands for Christ he is not weak

Not scared to preach on sin or hell

He's balanced and he teaches well

But first and foremost he is meant

To go wherever he is sent

His will is firmly tuned to God's

He walks by faith despite the odds

The love he shows one to another

Defines him as a solid Brother

"Destitute"

Wholly insufficient the utmost I can bring

My best and brightest attributes to them let me not cling

For if I bear a grunion, a mote, a scrap, a speck

Of anything that I did bring my motives I should check

He'll only fix what's broken the empty cup gets filled

O' wretched sinner that I am this carnal heart needs killed

I'm learning that my Saviour needs nothing I possess

For when I add me to Him I just make things a mess

Decrease me so I'm open right through me river flow

Living water right from You so others too may know

Lead me to Your purpose fill me with Your grace

Your mercy and compassion reflected on my face

And let me not forget this I beg of You Lord please

Remind me I stand strongest when down upon my knees

A broken beggar pleading O' Lord what can I do

My only worthy offering is leading men to you

So give me strength and courage for I have not my own

The greatest gift that I can share

That Your Name might be known

"Discovery"

Take my will and my life
And show me how to live
Guide me through the strife
And teach me how to give
Help me just to dwell
In the peace and love You bring
Make me only want
To do the next right thing
Guide me step by step
Lead me day by day
Teach me to accept
Your will along the way
Reveal to me all those
Who I damaged in the past
And help me make amends
And build friendships that will last
Let me learn to follow
That I may one day lead
Let not my life be hollow
But strong in word and deed
Thank You Lord for hearing me
I know You want what's best
Your Spirit in my heart
Has taught me these requests
And thank You for the iron
Deep down in my gut
The pulse that beats within and says
Don't use "NO MATTER WHAT!"

"Do the Deal"

Gravitation to the fact that I am but a man
A grounding force that binds my course according to God's plan
No matter where I wander or where my heart may roam
When pausing just to ponder "yep" this world is not my home
Distraction and frustration so easily embraced
I need to stop and pray my way through every challenge faced
Sometimes I feel like Jonah and I just want to run
But since the Truth has set me free I'm bound to seek the Son
His grip on me relentless so gentle yet so firm
He will not let me go you see no matter how I squirm
It really is a blessing to know He won't let go
Blessedly assuring me that I may truly know
His Spirit bears me witness no matter what I've done
That I have been adopted now called by Him a son
My mind can barely grasp it the measure of His love
From time to time I make the climb and glimpse what is above
Though usually I'm trudging along life's rocky way
The love He sheds within my heart quickens me each day
An attitude of gratitude my greatest saving grace
Reflecting on the light He shines that warms my weary face
He spareth no provision he maketh no mistake
My every need is met in Him when sleeping or awake
One more day unbroken is all I really need
And just my daily walk with Him may plant another seed
So many eyes are watching asking can this be for real
My lot in life to brave the strife and simply do the deal

"Do Work Son"

Extraordinary circumstances
A long and winding road
As sin increased until I ceased
To bear its heavy load
Relieved of that foul burden
Yet subject to its cause
For though I've been forgiven
My heart still has its flaws
As knowing leads to growing
It falls on me to look
To search my motivations out
And read them like a book
I wish it were that easy
But fear and pain collide
And fight my progress tooth and nail
Contending every stride
Apathetic laziness
Procrastination's twin
Would love to watch me lay around
And never ever win
But I was born to do great things
And so I must take heart
Smash that fear and grab a gear
Get started on my part
It may be pen to paper
Or service that needs done
Regardless I am capable
For God calls me His son

"Dreams"

Do you have a vision
A dream within your heart
A picture of what's possible
A calling to your part
For God has pre-determined
For each of us our roles
And if we choose not to obey
It complicates our souls
But if we heed His Spirit
Embracing Him for real
He'll fill us till we overflow
And cause our wounds to heal
Stand up for your convictions
Yes always do what's right
As God directs your every step
And fills your path with light
For even in the darkest valley
He is always there
His Spirit is inside you
He's with you everywhere
Don't give up on your dreams
No matter what they say
The world may be discouraged
But that is not God's way
His currency is hope and faith
Trust Him you will pull through
Keep your eyes on Christ my friend
For His dreams do come true

"Dust Storm"

The farthest far pavilions
Beneath the distant skies
Echo with the sounds of bombs
And wounded soldiers cries
There's danger in those deserts
Dark malice in those hills
With anger bred by ignorance
Eventually blood spills
There seems to be no logic
Nor purpose for man's hate
And death for disagreement
Seems to be the going rate
As if we have the knowledge
Much less the right to judge
When to take a human life
All to quench some grudge
It really begs the question
Can man know peace on earth
Will ever we have eyes to see
A human soul's true worth
This world has not the answers
With sin our hearts are flawed
And for this very purpose we
Must place our trust in God
I speak not of religion
In works we cannot trust
But only in the plan of Him
Who formed us from the dust

"E.R.D."

"Eternal Redemption Date"

Wasted days and wasted nights
Razor wire and bright flood lights
A six-by-nine a rock hard rack
The endless miles around the track
The work you do the pay you get
Is not enough to pay your debt
The drama and the politics
More of Satan's dirty tricks
There's so much selfish attitude
And some folks are just downright rude
If you let that stuff get you down
Your face will catch a perma-frown
A prison's full of hate and noise
And countless broken little boys
They're big and tough and mean and loud
And most of them are just too proud
They're too caught up in lies to see
That we all need humility
The truth is prison's not a curse
Cause things could really be much worse
And while we may not like it here
At least for now we can think clear
So take advantage of this time
To grow beyond a life of crime
There's only one way out of here
The Key to life is always near
So bend your knee and take His cup
Christ is the Way so just look up!

"Eternity"

The natural man he cannot see

He cannot grasp eternity

And when you simply try to tell

It's like trying to teach your ear how to smell

The lust of the flesh and the lust of the eyes

The pride of this life has him mesmerized

The devil's lie he has believed

He does not know he is deceived

He thinks this life is all there is

What he has he thinks it's his

He's trading it all for one little taste

He's going to fall O what a waste

Eternity goes on forever

But they are all so bloody clever

They think they'll cheat the Master's plan

But He will deal with every man

It does not have to be this way

But they care not for what we say

I hope and pray they see the light

Before that long eternal night

"Evil"

Evil is a sucker's bet
And you don't wanna pay that debt
Evil lurks within man's heart
Where pride and lust and greed doth start
The wicked thoughts that start within
When acted on then they are sin
A judgment made a hardness there
The moment we refuse to care
The stuff we do to serve our self
When we put God upon the shelf
Irreverence that's shown toward God
By evil is our thinking flawed
Yes at the fall the script got flipped
That was when our wings got clipped
There is a war that rages on
You need to know which side you're on
Sin and evil bring great pain
By it so many have been slain
These days people think it's cool
It's just a lie don't play the fool
The power that we need to win
Cannot be found in any sin
There's only One who holds the key
And what He has He gives for free
Break the spell and smash the lock
Stand with Christ He is the Rock!

"Face Time"

With a spike right through my shoulder
And a hinge inside my knee
I feel the ancient curse of man
A'creepin up on me
A bit more in the middle
And a little less on top
I used to go and never slow
But now I've learned to stop
A lot more in the planning
A bit less off the cuff
Amazingly I'm twice as free
Not caught up chasing stuff
I guess you'd say I'm wiser
I've learned to use my brain
And thinking things a good way through
Now saves me lots of pain
I actually feel pretty good
Despite my growing age
With confidence in Christ alone
I'll turn another page
No use in future trippin
The past has gone away
I'm simply grateful to the Lord
To live another day
But this much I can tell you
I hope against that day
When I will gaze upon His face
And all pain fades away

"Faces of Hope"

There seems to be a reason
For every trial in life
A purpose for each season
For all the pain and strife
It started out as just some fun
A way to pass the time
But kickin it got twisted quick
And ended up in crime
Just too much of a hassle
To follow every rule
Got no time for homework man
When you're too cool for school
Then soon enough the road gets tough
Cause now you're on your own
You can't be bothered with a job
When you're a rolling stone
Eventually you get caught up
Of that there is no doubt
For has it not been written friend
Your sin will find you out
Then all the glee and glamour
From tearing up the town
Falls on you like a hammer
When they come to take you down
You're tore up from the floor up

Admit it friend you're hooked
The inky finger shuffle
Then a mugshot and you're booked
The emotions you've been killing
Start coming home to roost
When you don't have your drug of choice
To give yourself a boost
My friend you've hit rock bottom
Yet things may turn out fine
Cause when you're at rock bottom
You can see the bottom line
It's time to make some changes
Let God into your heart
Ask Him where the Xchange is
It's an awesome place to start
To meet some other people
Who've been where you have been
Who've learned to trust in Jesus Christ
To overcome their sin
No matter your condition
Your grief your pain your loss
Day by day you'll find your way
Cause change starts at The Cross
Once He has restored you
And taught you how to cope
He'll send you out to change the world
A shining Face of Hope

"Faith"

Now faith is the substance of things hoped for
The evidence of things not seen
Fully Assured I Trust Him
To wash me completely clean
Through faith we know the worlds were framed
Alone by the Word of God
While those who doubt can't understand
To them it sounds too odd
There's only one way to get it or haven't you heard
Faith cometh by hearing and that by the Word
Yes faith is the mortar that locks in each stone
Even so without works it's dead when alone
Noah had faith and Moses did too
They trusted in God to carry them through
From faith to faith is God's nature revealed
By it the Saints are strengthened and healed
The just shall live by it for so it is written
While many are lost for with doubt they are smitten
Through faith in His Word His grace He will give
If we simply believe then forever we'll live
You can't please Him without it that's just how it goes
But diligent seekers and believers He knows
So if you have faith keep it and love it
For Christ is the Author and Finisher of it

"Faithful"

Faithful is the servant who
Walks within Your way
He lives to serve You Father God
Each and every day
Early in the morning or late into the night
It matters not the time or place
He lives to shine Your light
When asked to give a reason
For the hope within his heart
Let his words convey Your love
Right from the very start
Let him show Your mercy Lord
Yes let him share Your grace
That he may see in every man
The need to see Your face
Help him share Your story Lord all along the way
Appoint to him a needy ear each and every day
And let his heart be ready Lord sanctify his tongue
Your Gospel freely pouring out
That bell won't be un-rung
And let him hold Your promise
Lord deep within his soul
That You will finish that good work
Which makes him right and whole
Give him strength and courage Lord
To stand for what is right
Guide him on Your narrow way
And lead him by Your light
But most of all remind him Lord
That in You we are One
Members of the Body of
Your precious Holy Son

"Fear Not"

The laying down of worries
The folding of the hands
Fear Not is not suggested
It's one of God's commands
No matter what I'm doing
No matter where I go
High above He watches me
And walks with me below
His Holy Scripture tells me
Exactly who I am
A blood bought son and servant
The price paid by The Lamb
And so I will rejoice in Him
It brings my heart great peace
The wonders of His blessings
May wonders never cease
His calm and quiet spirit
Life's every storm bestills
My every need supplied indeed
From atop a thousand hills
It's not just love and mercy
There's strength and power too
Christ strengthens me to go and be
His hands in all I do
So take heart now my brethren
For worry is a sin
I've read the final chapter
The Bible says We Win!

"Flow"

Contentment still eludes me
I know I can do more
Believe, perceive and then achieve
That's what God saved me for
To serve my King regardless
Of how it makes me feel
To give without receiving
Upon the potter's wheel
I feel His fingers stretching me
With gentle strength so firm
His plan and purpose for my life
Prevails though I may squirm
I know not why I do resist
The changes that He makes
For every circumstance in life
He's chosen for our sakes
So who am I to question why
My place is to accept
To simply grow and always know
That in His heart I'm kept
And so I must remember
No matter where I go
To simply open up my heart
And let His Spirit flow

"Focus"

Reach me teach me give me sight

Guide me by Your shining light

Scold me hold me mold me true

Grow me up to look like You

Scourge from me the lust and pride

Root it out from deep inside

Wash me with Your Holy Word

Reprove me of the lies I've heard

Give to me a heart that's true

And only seeks what comes from You

Prompt me to do my very best

Give me a thirst to live with zest

And when I see a heart in need

Teach me to plant Your precious seed

Give to me the words to say

And lead me Father when I pray

Thank You Lord for hearing me

In Jesus Name let these things be

"Forgiveness"

Forgiveness is holy forgiveness is true
For when you forgive it cleanses you
To err it is human to forgive is divine
And a heart that forgives is clearly a sign
A sign that you've been to the cross and you've seen
Through the Lord's eyes and what He did mean
When He said forgive them they know not what they do
Their minds are deceived and they have not a clue
Forgiven by God means I'm justified
As if I'd never stolen or hated or lied
It means I've been pardoned my sins are washed clean
No better than you if you know what I mean
And since I'm forgiven I must learn to forgive
For that is the Spirit in which we must live
To walk in His presence and dwell in His grace
To have only love for every last face
Forgiveness is also to give ourselves too
Don't beat yourself up for the things that you do
Forgive and forget move on and keep going
In the garden of God we forgive to keep growing
Remember my friends that truly to live
As we've been forgiven we must learn to forgive

(Matthew 6:14-15)

"Fortress"

Your architecture's attitude is strong and straight and true
An edifice of spirit stones firmly laid by You
The plumbline of Your Word is that which levels out each stone
Generations jointly locked none standing on their own
Decades in the forming each block is hewn with care
Faith the mortar locking in each piece exactly where
You the Master Builder would have our place to be
Supported and supporting others which we do not see
Foundational in nature each row supports the next
Built upon preceding generations it protects
Carpenter of carpenters the Cornerstone we need
Humble Your beginning as the tiny mustard seed
Yet what a mighty bulwark standing up within this world
Upon the battlements Your banner's been unfurled
Let every spot and blemish from Your bride now be removed
In spite of persecutions she's always been improved
Though the past is now behind us the future yet to come
Firmly we are standing jointly locked and true to plumb
Are the capstones now among us is the time now drawing near
That's really not for us to know that's one thing You made clear
Let not our present troubles be that to which we cling
But trumpet from the rooftops let Your Gospel clearly ring

"Freedom"

Freedom what it means to me
I thought I knew till recently
The things I thought were really cool
Were just the things to tempt a fool
Like chasing girls and doing dope
Whatever else to help me cope
Like diamond rings and muscle cars
Hot rod bikes and loud guitars
The pleasure that I got from these
Increased the depth of my disease
I fought and stole and lied and killed
I did not care whose blood got spilled
My world was fast and dark and bleak
I fed upon the lost and weak
They'd lose their kids and rob their mother
Just to pay this faulty brother
I thought I was a solid guy
But that was just another lie
Eventually I made the joint
Ten times before I got the point
I always thought my way was best
And every time I failed the test
The things I did to serve my self

Set me back upon the shelf
I'd left my job my kids my wife
To live a lonesome prison life
I used to value flesh and gold
But all of that gets really old
I'm tired of lust and hate and scorn
All those things just leave me torn
Deep down inside I have a space
A yearning for love's warm embrace
I'm made that way you know it's true
Deep down inside you have one too
There's only One who holds the key
To know Him is to be set free
He'll fill your joy and mend your heart
In Him you'll have a brand new start
The things you used to do and say
Will be no more they've passed away
He'll guide your path and give you sight
To spread His news and shine His light
He'll feed you daily with His Word
To go teach others what you've heard
He'll lead you on His narrow way
Give you a cross to bear each day
I am a lock and He's the Key
I serve the Rock and now I'm free!

"Freeride"

A kick a cough
A rumble and I'm off
A flash of chrome
The road my second home
A long black ribbon that splits the land
The thunder cracks at twist of hand
The rumbling pipes beneath my seat
As stripes flash by my booted feet
The apes that frame my carefree course
Chrome reins they are to guide this horse
A bedroll for a makeshift bed
A borrowed floor to lay my head
And what won't fit within my bags
Got no use that stuff just drags
A tank of gas
A rocky mountain pass
A blessed ride
Along the ocean side
The Way the Truth
The Life that is the proof
A horse a sword
A rider for the Lord

"Friends"

What a friend is supposed to do
Is have your back and talk to you
Tell you when you're out of line
Remind you things will turn out fine
Talk you down when you get high
Always look you in the eye
What they have they give you half
And they can always make you laugh
And even when you act a fool
Deep down inside you know it's cool
Cause even when you're at your worst
They always put your feelings first
But what true friends are most of all
A hand to lift you when you fall
These are some things within my heart
Where I feel true friends should start
Friends are forever right to the end
I'm glad to say that you're my friend

"Glimpses"

These dreams that come
They strike me dumb
I utter not a word
Even if I were to speak
These things you've never heard
The things that I imagine
The visions that He sends
A life of love and laughter
Amongst so many friends
For when they finally happen
Yes once they come to pass
It dawns on me 'twas just a glimpse
As through a looking glass
It seems to be what He shows me
A tiny piece at best
A promise that my heart can hold
Till He shows me the rest
For once I'm in the moment
And living it for real
There's always so much more to see
Than glimpses can reveal
So when God gives you vision
Within your heart accept
That every promise ever made
By Him is surely kept

"Glory to Glory"

It's all the little things
They add up to much more
Than all the lofty goals
I'm always striving for
To get a good night's sleep
And wake up feeling blessed
To lay me down at night
Relaxed and not so stressed
Hot water in the shower
Some gas to drive my car
And oh so nice to have a job
That's really not too far
And man it's really nice
To always pack a smile
I take it with me everywhere
Mile after mile
But so far just this week
The greatest joy as yet
To simply sit and speak
To a brother that I met
To see that knowing nod
The light upon his face
As we simply spoke of God
Both spirits bathed in grace
Yes all the little things
I'm grateful for each one
The sweet smell of the roses
The gorgeous rising sun
I know these are those glories
That Paul was speaking of
When he picked up the pen and wrote
Of God's unending love

"Good News"

From Eve to final trumpet's call
Upon His knees He took it all
Great drops of sweat did fall as blood
As anguish from our sins did flood
Beneath that tree where serpent hissed
Betrayer's lips our Saviour kissed
And that the mob dared not in light
With staves and swords they did at night
From there on hallowed holy ground
The Prince of Peace was taken bound
Those very ones He called His own
Had wicked minds and hearts of stone
Mocked and scorned and beaten there
They spit on Him tore out His hair
Accusing Him with every breath
Their only aim to cause His death
So on to Pilate He was bound
Who in Him said "there's no fault found"
But gnashing teeth and frenzied crowd
Called for the death of Him aloud
They cried "upon us His blood be"
God's love and truth they could not see
To prove that he was Caesar's friend
To scourge and Cross did Pilate send
Thirty nine the lashes ripped
As from His frame the flesh was stripped
Mockery and insults stormed
As for His brow a crown was formed

No gold, no jewels, just blood and thorn
From sin cursed ground His brow was torn
Then on to Calvary He trod
That perfect sinless Son of God
Falling down along the way
He showed to us that very day
That two are stronger than just one
As Simon came and helped His Son
A picture on salvation's road
He sends us help to bear the load
How desolate that mountain top
His mortal body's final stop
As iron spikes were driven in
The grisly biting sting of sin
His Cross then lifted high above
Held not by nails instead by love
While dying there He made His plea
"Forgive them for they cannot see"
Betrayed and rejected, condemned and forsaken
All simply so my place could be taken
My sin debt to hell paid off in full
Crimson dark stain now snow white as wool
The Lamb of God was slain that day
For when there's sin there's hell to pay
But He who laid His own life down
Did rise again and wears a crown
For though death has a bitter sting
It could not hold our precious King
He's seated now at God's right hand
Go share this News is His command

"Grace"

God's riches at Christ's expense
The mercy He shows despite my offense
By it we are saved through faith of course
When we come to Him with a heart of remorse
He tells us come boldly come now to this place
That we may obtain mercy from His throne of grace
Though sin taints us all and does simply confound
How much more does His grace surely abound
When He became flesh and dwelt among us
Full of grace and of truth is what His glory was
The words of our mouth should be loud and clear
To minister grace to all those who hear
His grace is sufficient and He gives to the humble
And extra He gives whenever we stumble
Daily we ask Him in grace let us grow
Open our eyes so Your face we will know
By it we are called not for works we have done
But simply because we are loved every one
God's grace is a case of unmerited favour
For it is the reason He sent us a Saviour
The Father is love and He knew what it meant
When into the world was His only Son sent
He knew the blood price that Jesus would pay
For He wrote the law that even He must obey
So remember my friends when you see His face
That your ticket home is His free gift of grace

"Gratitude"

I'm overwhelmed by love sometimes
I feel just downright blessed
For when I see what God gives me
I'm really quite impressed
Just let me count my blessings now
And name them one by one
First and foremost my best Friend
Our Father's precious Son
And then there is His Spirit
So deep down in my heart
Shedding love from high above
Reminding me I'm part
Part of His creation
His story and His song
This confirmation in my soul
Keeps me standing strong
I'm grateful for this planet
That God would think of me
Creating such magnificence
A place for me to be
I'm grateful for my loved ones
My family and my friends
And for the chance to share my hope
With new folks that He sends
I'm grateful for this nation

Despite its many flaws
I'm proud that we defend the weak
A just and noble cause
I'm blessed to have a legal way
To earn my daily bread
So grateful God transformed my life
Before I wound up dead
I'm grateful I have air to breath
Cool water I can drink
I'm also glad to wash with it
Or else I'd really stink
I'm grateful for my problems
That I've been taught to face
Instead of running off to hide
I meet them by God's grace
I'm grateful for the talent
To share these words with you
And for God's Spirit in your heart
Confirming they are true
And I am very grateful for
God's joy and peace and rest
Assuring me eternity
Among His very best
But if I should lose sight of that
Forgetting my own place
Most of all I'm grateful for
God's boundless perfect grace

"Happy Mother's Day"

When my life first got its start
And I could hear your beating heart
I knew nothing of this world
For in you I was safely curled
But soon you would know pain and strife
As you brought forth this son to life
The agony you felt that day
You gladly bore to make a way
For me to grow and be a man
From pain comes life that is God's plan
You fed me clothed me kept me warm
Gave me shelter from life's storm
You taught me things that I should know
To make me strong and help me grow
Now many years have passed away
I've known some trials but that's okay
It makes no difference where I go
I love you Mom you need to know
The things I've said the stuff I've done
Regardless I am still your son
A blessing from the Lord above
To know you as the Mom I love
Thank you Mom for all you've done
I thank the Lord that I'm your son

Happy Mother's Day
I Love You Mom
Love James

"Happy New Year"

It's January first today
Another year has passed away
The last one was the best one yet
I'm almost done I've paid my debt
The day to go is drawing near
I'm finally going home this year
I've learned so much this time around
My feet are firmly on the ground
I've spent some time upon my knees
The Lord hears all my heartfelt pleas
He's taught me well and strengthened me
Bought me from hell and set me free
He has restored my broken life
I pray He also heals my wife
I'm looking forward to this year
I have no doubts I have no fear
I know In Him I can do all things
No matter what this old world brings
With Him to guide I will stand tall
I vow to ride from wall to wall
Preaching to the brethren there
My life poured out for now I care
There are so many left inside

For them He also lived and died
I feel my Lord is sending me
To go and set the captives free
To ride for Him across the land
With His Bible in my hand
An Iron Saint I ask to be
Serving You and riding free
I'll stay the course and go the length
As long as You provide the strength
One last prayer Lord hear my plea
When sending forth Lord please send me

"Heartbeat"

My heart is simply bursting
With all I'd like to say
I simply don't know where to start
But each and every day
I'll tell you that I love you
And that I really mean it
And even though you'll hear it
You'll know it cause you've seen it
I pledge my sworn allegiance
No matter what I do
To honor and respect you
And love you through and through
The Father is revealing
How true His love can be
Through the heart He's given you
That you now give to me
My prayer is He will give us
Many years of joy
Loving one another
Whilst engaged in His employ
Two solid souldier servants blended into one
A three bound cord that wraps the sword
Held by God's own Son
I pray that He will use us
To shine His brilliant light
A precious prime example
Of how to do things right
May blessings and prosperity

Flow freely from our hands
As we walk in victory
And honor His commands
I love how much you love Him
It's very plain to see
It's how I know how real you are
When you say you love me
I'm learning and I'm growing
To be a better man
I do believe and so receive
This chapter of His plan
The stuff of fairytales
Is what this romance is
An epic love affair of hearts
Firmly tuned to His
Truly madly deeply unquenchably ignit
The fire of our spirits
By His they have been lit
My words though true and honest
Are just not quite enough
They don't describe this feeling
It's really kind of tough
I guess I'll have to show you
A thousand different ways
How much I really love you
Right till the end of days

Tiffany Gabrielle Alexis Edens I Love You

"Held"

Tomorrow is not promised
And yesterday is gone
So focus on this day and pray
For strength to carry on
No use in future tripping
Or pining for the past
For houses built on sand are simply
Destined not to last
Each moment in your lifetime is
A precious gift from God
Each breath a miracle itself
Magnificence unflawed
The fact that I can think then move
Astounding truth be known
As God controls the heavens
All while seated on the throne
Yet though He turns the planets
And holds each grain of sand
The heart which beats within my breast
Does so at His command
All things by Him created
His will that they exist
And seen or not He holds the lot
By Him all things consist
(Colossians 1:16-17)

"His Cup"

Go to Him O weary one
He'll set you free He is the Son
And like a bird with broken wing
He'll mend your heart teach you to sing
There'll be no wait He'll see you first
A sip from Him will quench your thirst
The Bread He breaks and gives to eat
Will fill you up and taste so sweet
He'll wipe your tears and wash you clean
He'll show you things you've never seen
The strength He gives will help you cope
And what He says will give you hope
His courage He will bring and share
He'll fill your heart with love and care
His gift of life He'll give to you
But first you have to ask Him to
Salvation is a full sweet cup
It's up to you to pick it up

"His Love"

Higher than the heavens
Deeper than the sea
Greater is the love
Which my Saviour has for me
Who shall come between us
Shall trials or distress
Or any sword or perils
Or even nakedness
And as it has been written
Even though we may be killed
Through Him we're more than victors
And with His love we're filled
For I have been persuaded
That nothing ever made
Can take me from my Saviour
Or beat the price He paid
His love transcends creation
He's saved us from the fall
Our Master's love is calling
Will you heed the Masters call?

(Romans 8:35-39)

"His Name"

Drawn out from the heathen
Gathered from afar
It matters not what men call you
For God knows who you are
Cleansed from all your idols
From filthiness made clean
A new and tender heart transformed
From stony cold and mean
His Spirit will instill in you
That bright and shining light
That only seeks to know His will
And do that which is right
And we shall be His people
And He shall be our God
And great the comfort we enjoy
By His staff and rod
So great is His provision
No famine to us known
Of His increase there is no cease
No need for bread from stone
All of this He does for us
Despite our guilt and shame
That no man living can deny
The power of His Name
(Ezekiel 36:24-38)

"His Story"

Twas light the night when He was born
Twas dark the day His flesh was torn
When coming in and going out
Two miracles to cast out doubt
A borrowed crib a borrowed tomb
An empty grave a virgin womb
An angel at His head and feet
Within that tomb the mercy seat
On Sinai was our sin explained
While Calvary washed white the stained
Creation it was signed and sealed
And judgment day will be revealed
First came the Lamb He died in pain
The Lion will in glory reign
Of all these things we have been told
The greatest one will soon unfold
The dies been cast it's set in stone
Yes quickly we shall see His throne
So come Lord Jesus to this place
That we may see Your shining face

"Maranatha"

"Holy Spirit"

When we open up our heart
And ask God for a brand new start
There may be nothing that is felt
But at that point we are indwelt
Yes Someone comes to live within
The moment we are born-again
If we pray daily to be filled
So much will come it will get spilled
Out of us it flows to others
Turning our enemies into our brothers
By its holy power we are each healed
Till the day of redemption with it we're sealed
It wakes us up and keeps us going
Within each heart its force is flowing
Without it there would be no life
It carries us through trials and strife
It comforts us and leads us true
And gives us strength to make it through
But like an athlete that gets benched
When we don't heed it, it is quenched
And when we sin you best believe it
Brother you can sorely grieve it
But listen close and you will hear it
I'm speaking of God's Holy Spirit

"Honesty"

Honesty transcends our talk
More than words it's how we walk
Integrity in all we do
What other people think of you
It's standing on your own two feet
And what you start you do complete
And while it's never telling lies
It's also shunning compromise
It's telling friends just what you see
It is accountability
And what you owe you always pay
It's putting in a full workday
It's making sure you've done your part
It's asking God to search your heart
And when He's searched you through and through
It's doing what he tells you to
But most of all it's being real
And if you're His it is His seal

"Hope"

There is a thing that helps us to cope
We look to it and call it hope
Within God's Word we have been told
Exactly how things will unfold
And though this world is full of strife
Beyond it waits eternal life
And while things may seem quite unfair
We wait to meet Christ in the air
The devil's deeds may cause a frown
But Christ will give to us a crown
And while this world is full of sin
God's Word tells us we shall win
And everything we have been told
From His Word's as good as gold!!!!
(Proverbs 30:5)

"Hopeful"

Hope values things promised
Hope knows in the end
All will be well for we have a Friend
Hope sees past problems
Hope has no doubt
Hope knows regardless things will work out
Hope powers the pilgrim to keep pressing in
Hope comes from knowing that one day we'll win
But hope can be fragile for it can be lost
When up on the waves of this life one is tossed
A promise from God that is the seed
Watered with faith it grows like a weed
My hope it is better than pleasure or money
When my hopes are fulfilled
They'll be sweeter than honey
When my hopes are met
I'll see em and know em
But for now I'm just hoping
That you like this poem

"Humble Pie"

In peeling back the layers which
Surround my selfish heart
I'm painfully reminded that
I must own my part
I'm told that I must look upon
The things of others too
Considering my neighbors place
And not just what they do
A chance to know the mind of Christ
And not put my self first
To banish murder from my heart
Resentments are the worst
I pray that God will give me strength
To stay calm and be cool
To live a life that's free from strife
And walk His golden rule
The greatest thing I could achieve
To just get out the way
Then maybe others could believe
There's truth in what I say
I guess I need a whole lot more
Of Him and less of me
For faith in Christ and Him alone
Will set a sinner free

"I Feel Ya"

Walking by faith not stumbling by sight

Trusting the Lord and the power of His might

Abandoned rejected so cold and alone

My life's greatest pains my Saviour has known

For He has felt hatred and He has known scorn

And the pain that He knew left Him broken and torn

In all ways was He tempted and so He can say

I've been there my child I've felt the same way

His faith in the Father brought Him through whole

And faith in His grace brings peace to my soul

"I Wish"

I wish I were a piece of gold
So shiny and so fine
Treated better than where I used to live
In a dark and muddy mine
I wish I were an eagle
Soaring through the sky
Seeking out my prey
With my A-1 eagle eye
I wish I were a sunbeam
Shining out through space
And coming down and warming
A sweet and gentle face
I wish I were a singer
That I could sing a song
Its words would make you happy
And its wisdom make you strong
I wish you could see clearly
How much we could set right
You know I love you dearly
Let me lead you to the light
I wish you knew my Father
I wish you could be won
You wonder why I bother
So you might know the Son

"Immanuel"

This story was written a long time ago
So people like us would all one day know
The Way and the Truth and the Life of the One
Our Lord and our Saviour God's own Holy Son
Nearly eight hundred years before Christ walked the earth
The prophet Isaiah foretold of His birth
He told of a Son that a virgin would bear
That crazy old prophet with long flowing hair
He said they would name Him Immanuel
He'd set free His people and keep them from hell
The child of a woman and the Son of our God
The King of all kings come to walk on this sod
He gave us a list of the Names they would use
Wonderful, Counselor, King of the Jews
The High Mighty God, The Prince of all Peace
The Remover of sins from the west to the east
Then many years passed and finally one day
The archangel Gabriel was sent down to say
Hail maid Mary blessed are ye
Thou art highly favoured and the Lord is with thee
He said she'd been chosen to bear in her womb
The High Son of God though she'd known not a groom
With wonder and awe she asked how can this be
He said God's Holy Ghost shall come upon thee
And when she had heard this and humbly agreed
God sent His Spirit to bring her His Seed
She had promised Joseph that they would be married
And he knew that it was not his child that she carried

But he was a good man and his mercy was ample
Not willing to make her a public example
Though he was of a mind to send her away
The angel of God had something to say
While Joseph was sleeping the angel appeared
Said this woman is blessed be not a feared
The Child she carries must be not abhorred
As a matter of fact He's a Gift from the Lord
I want you to raise Him as if He were your son
But know in your heart He's the true Promised One
Name Him Yeshua when He arrives
For He shall be Saviour to so many lives
Then many months later a star in the sky
Drew men from the east whom they called the Magi
They came to see Herod and brought him the news
We're seeking a Child the King of the Jews
So they left Herod's court by the star were they led
On to Bethlehem town also called House of Bread
Gifts they came bearing such as gold that was pure
Sweet smelling incense and for His burial myrrh
When they entered the house and saw the young King
They bowed down and worshipped and angels did sing
While shepherds were tending their flocks on that night
Shining down on them came brilliant white light
The angel said fear not I bring great tidings of joy
This night a Saviour is born a sweet Baby Boy
They saw heavenly multitudes praising and then
They heard peace on the earth and good will toward all men

(Merry Christmas)

"In the Wind"

The daily grind that numbs the mind

The endless strife that sucks the life

You sweat and strive just to survive

You work and slave to an early grave

There's got to be a better way

A way to get free and play

You still have time to change your course

And get yourself an iron horse

Some steel and chrome a place to roam

Some thick black leather some decent weather

The sun the hills the open road

Some fun to kill life's heavy load

Your bank account screams you have sinned

But Brother can you feel that wind

You've worked real hard and paid your debt

You bought this steed with blood and sweat

This is the way a life should be

So spread your wings come ride with me

"In the Yard"

As sprinklers like maracas
Sing cha cha on the lawn
A gentle green spring evening
Quietly flows on
The birds are sweetly singing
Amidst the tender leaves still new
What this pleasant scene is bringing
Are longing thoughts of you
The orchards that surround me
Are blossoming white blooms
Heralding the harvest
Which in the future looms
The rumble in the distance
Of a brother riding by
He's likely just out riding
And he needs no reason why
Just now I shared this poem
I read it to a guard
Yes that's right my friend
I wrote this in the yard

"Iron On Iron"

Faithful are the wounds of a friend

For they are meant to heal not to rend

When brothers take great care

In how and what they share

The Spirit gives His seal

And makes their words more real

For meekness is the key

To help a brother see

The things he needs to know

To help him learn and grow

And if that brother hears

It may save him many tears

So when your brothers do their part

Heed their words within your heart

For they are wise they know the score

That's what we have our brothers for

"James"

James you are My special child
Your former life was fast and wild
But everything that you went through
My hand of grace it covered you
I chastened you when you were wrong
I strengthened you and made you strong
I've carried you through toils and strife
And drawn you to My gift of life
Slowly I am changing you
To make you solid pure and true
I've turned your mind to things above
And taught you how to truly love
I've put in you a heart to preach
And honed your mind to learn and teach
I wash you daily with My Word
Now go tell others what you've heard
Along the way you must prepare
And start each day with solemn prayer
Let me take your lust and pride
And teach you how to just abide
Know you are My precious one
I love you James you are My son

"Jarhead"

Another day of living out
The dream that is my life
There's no compare to back there where
Each day was filled with strife
The gift of good clean livin
'Tis more than I deserve
And oh the priceless blessing just
To simply go and serve
Each battle fought and won is not
By hammer axe or sword
I simply stand in victory
Depending on the Lord
No need to ever worry now
My faith has made me whole
For God has shed His grace on me
And spared my mortal soul
Now if I get the chance to go
And share a little hope
It may just be the golden key
To help somebody cope
For in the darkest valley deep
A little light may shine
And who knows if those trodden down
Had just asked for a sign
We call it confirmation
Miraculous no doubt
A vessel for Your message Lord
So please just pour me out

"Jesus Alone"

Jesus alone saves me from death

Jesus alone gives me each breath

Jesus alone shows me the Way

Jesus alone leads me each day

Jesus alone teaches me right

Jesus alone shines on me light

Jesus alone He is the Source

Jesus alone He sets my course

Jesus alone He takes my hand

Jesus alone in Him do I stand

Jesus alone gives me His love

Jesus alone shall take me above

Jesus alone He is the Stone

Jesus alone Jesus alone

"Joshua"

Joshua Joshua how you are named
The way home to heaven is what here is claimed
Listen young brother to what I tell you
Your name is of old and ancient Hebrew
Jehovah is saviour is what it doth mean
Tis the name of His Son for He washes us clean
Be strong and courageous is what he was told
That first Joshua in the Testament Old
With the Lord in his heart and a sword in his hand
He led his whole nation to their promised land
Yes God is salvation is what it doth mean
So stay strong and pure and keep yourself clean
Your name is a gift from the Father to you
Just like His Son which He gave for you too
Jesus Yeshua while not quite the same
Means the same thing as your very name
So love it respect it do what is right
Stay on the path and walk in the light
Remember my brother that life's not a game
The answer to all is contained in your name

"Judgment"

Standing there before His throne

So small and naked and alone

There's no place left to hide your face

You've no excuse for squandered grace

Your selfish acts and idle boasts

Laid bare before the Lord of Hosts

The fire in His piercing eyes

Incinerates your web of lies

And there beneath His brazen feet

Sin is judged its end complete

The dead will be there great and small

And by their works He'll judge them all

You still have time to change your fate

Just ask Him in it's not too late

For if you keep a heart of stone

You'll stand before His great white throne

"Just Do"

A simple act of kindness is
The best thing when it's true
When done for nothing other than
The next right thing to do
Not done to gain one's favor
Or for the crowd's applause
Nor from a guilty conscience
Based on religious laws
But simply and sincerely
Straight up right from the heart
That's the stuff of character
To play that little part
That little part of God's own plan
For His love to be shown
Your actions His reflection
That His Son may be known
For you may be the only Christ
That some folks ever see
And hopefully your actions
Give them hope to be set free
A curious attraction
Compelling on its own
That little spark of Spirit
From God through you is shown
So keep it simple Christian
But please make sure it's true
Don't run ahead and try too much
Just do what you can do

"King of Kings"

The eye of the beholder
Is where the beauty lies
A heart believes and so perceives
Much stronger than the eyes
For what one's heart holds dearest
May not be dear to you
But to the heart that's nearest
That love is strong and true
For is not what you treasure
That thing for which you yearn
The master of your heart of hearts
Or will it simply burn
Doth moth or rust corrupt it
Is it something one could steal
Or will it wilt and die someday
Or is it even real
There's so much to consider
So many different things
Yet nothing holds a candle to
My Christ the King of Kings

"Kinsman Redeemer"

My Kinsman Redeemer so willing so just

You took on this form that was a must

You know how it feels to live and to die

Not some distant Spirit up in the sky

My Kinsman Redeemer my Saviour my King

My Lord and my God my Everything

You cleansed the earth with Your awesome flood

As You cleanse my soul with Your precious Blood

My Kinsman Redeemer my Teacher my Master

All other paths will lead to disaster

For You are the Truth the Life and the Way

And You guide my steps day after day

My Kinsman Redeemer my Daddy my Friend

Of Your love and grace there is no end

You have redeemed me you made me whole

My Jesus The Christ Lover of my soul

"Knowing"

Standing on the promises that Your Word gives to me
Walking tall despite the fall and claiming victory
My faith means I believe You right down to Your last word
Not caught up in confusion from anything I've heard
Affirmation from my walk is what I do enjoy
When from Your statutes wisdom is what I do employ
You've given me a roadmap within Your sacred text
The faith that You are with me my heart and mind protects
How blessed the assurance that by You I am known
Adopted to your family a son You call Your own
There is no man made problem nor creature great or small
Strong enough to separate You vanquish one and all
Yet if I think I've got this and forget that I need You
I'm doomed to repeat failures I will not make it through
For only when I'm walking with my hand placed in Yours
Not trying to control things or settle petty scores
Will Your peace fill my spirit and give me such a lift
And keep me firmly grounded so that I do not drift
No longer ruled by chaos and tossed by crashing waves
But knowing in my spirit that only Jesus saves
A blessing just to know this and know that this alone
His blood the only reason my name is by the Father known

"Known"

A common misconception
You see it every day
So many have convinced themselves
There is some other way
To make it into heaven
Or not end up in hell
They've been deceived and do believe
The liar's wicked spell
It's such a murky mixture
Emotions, thoughts, and pride
It blinds men to the cold hard fact
That God came down and died
It really is quite simple
We need Him cause we're broke
And all the other rubbish
Is merely mirrors and smoke
None of it has substance
No matter what you've heard
The only thing that you can trust
Is God's unchanging Word
It tells us grass will wither
And flowers fade away
While His Word stands forever
And perfect it will stay
It does not need defending
The truth stands on its own
And greater peace cannot be had
Than when His truth is known

"Learning to Lean"

Growing into knowing and learning more each day
I'm absolutely mesmerized all along the way
As wisdom slowly coalesces things appear to me
While strongholds crack and crumble my spirit is set free
Old fears are growing weaker as my faith is multiplied
For every trial and trap I've met solutions were supplied
I'd like to say success was mine through every one of these
But sometimes through my failures am I given wisdom's keys
Sometimes the greatest lessons
Come through error or through sin
Yet how much more rewarding
When they come from pressing in
Striving ever onward all along this narrow way
The point is not perfection but progression every day
It isn't always easy as much effort is required
And forging through the maze of life can leave one feeling tired
Yet this I know down here below
This world is not my home
No matter where I find myself
Or where my feet may roam
As loneliness besets me the short term may look grim
But Christ prepares my mansion and so I follow Him
I don't have all the answers but I know the One who does
You ask me why I trust Him and I tell you just because
He's brought me through so much intact
And sheltered me from harms
Yes growing into knowing how to lean upon His arms

"Lessons"

Deep inside within my soul
There is a yawning aching hole
A vacuum void I cannot fill
Like water running down a hill
And strangely all that draws me in
Binding chords which lead to sin
The endless quest will never cease
And never ever bring true peace
It seems the shiny pretty things
Pack the painfullest of stings
It's not that beauty is not good
Oh' that my heart worked as it should
A wretched sinner I was born
My selfish soul already torn
I did not need a lesson one
To lie or steal or live for fun
Yet each mistake I've ever made
With pain was my tuition paid
And never heeding sound advice
That foolishness exacts a price
I treasure now each lesson learned
Yes even those where I got burned
I pray to be a wiser man
Relinquishing my own flawed plan
And since we know God answers prayer
Maybe I'm already there
Not sure why the Father does
Just grateful I'm not where I was

"Life Lessons"

Overcoming obstacles every single day
Knowing God allows the trials I find along the way
Staying in the Spirit the best way that I know
To navigate successfully and in so doing grow
Acknowledging my failures examining my flaws
Incongruent actions versus universal laws
Rules for righteous living are meant to prosper me
And only through obedience may I be truly free
Knowing these dynamics and believing that they're true
God's compass meant to guide me that I may make it through
My wounds are self-inflicted of this there is no doubt
I've proven time and time again my sin will find me out
I need to heed the lessons that God is teaching me
Paying close attention that I may clearly see
He's working all together for that which is the best
In faith I must remember this and just discard the rest
My hope to be found worthy in everything I do
The man who God intended right and strong and true
And only through His power do I have any hope
To walk that straight and narrow path or merely even cope
May gratitude be magnified may this heart be content
That I may have discernment to know just what He meant
Each white-capped crashing wave each ripple that He gives
Are movements that He sends me to remind me Jesus Lives!

"Love"

Though I speak as a man with an angel's sweet voice
If I have not love then I'm just making noise
And though I have knowledge and gifts from on high
If I have not love then nothing am I
Though I bestow on the poor all the good that I've got
If I have not love it profits me not
Love suffers long and is kind without pride
Vaunts not itself has no envy inside
Behaves not unseemly seeks not her own
Is patient when picked on evil thoughts are unknown
Finds no joy in sin but rejoices in right
Bears all things with hope and stands in the light
Love never fails when all else falls short
Like the wisdom of men or a false prophet's report
For now we know pieces but we are not sure
But when the Son cometh shall our knowledge be pure
When I was young I'd run and I'd play
But now as a man I've put that stuff away
For now I see darkly till I see His face
Then will I realize the full measure of grace
Till then I abide in faith hope and love
These three priceless gifts from the Lord up above
The faith and the hope while they come from me
They're merely reflections of God's charity
(1 Corinthians 13)

"Make a Wish"

Would you like to make a wish
And have that wish come true
Then listen up my friend
And I will tell you what to do
Just set your mind on things above
Not on those things that perish
Let your heart be filled with love
That ye may ever cherish
His Spirit that now lives in you
Will guide you in all things
And you will grow to know and love
The peace His presence brings
The world the flesh the devil
Will try to bring you down
The culmination of the curse
That wretched thorny crown
But from the pain inflicted
That agony endured
Our hopelessness was overcome
Our lost condition cured
Delight yourself in Him my friend
His Good News spread anew
Just plant His seeds and pray He feeds
And watch your wish come true

"Matthew"

Matthew my Brother listen to me
I'll teach you a lesson and give you a key
To know what it means when you hear your name
Gift of Jehovah it doth proclaim
To most of the world it might seem quite odd
But to all of the Saints it means gift of God
The Saint you're named after was quite a rich man
Till he left all behind to follow God's plan
The Gospel he wrote was meant to help save us
Another true gift that God simply gave us
He followed our Lord and walked with the Brothers
He poured out his life a servant to others
The Gospel he wrote shows Jesus as King
How He gave us His all poured out everything
It's not just a name but why you were sent
A life lived for God couldn't be better spent
So remember next time when you need a lift
You're not just a man but you are God's gift
His gift to the world to your parents and brothers
But His greatest gift is what you do for others
Matthew my Brother what I tell you is right
Forsake every other and stay in the light
Yes gift of Jehovah is what it doth mean
The name you were given so keep yourself clean

"Mind of Christ"

When putting on the mind of Christ one must remember this
He prayed for those who did Him wrong this thing we must not miss
Please forgive them Father for they know not what they do
Now that love's unconditional and sees what's right and true
The problem with deception they don't know they're deceived
But all that was revealed to me the hour I first believed
It's really hard to pray for all the haters who heap scorn
But was this not the reason that our Saviour's flesh was torn
Growth comes with submission beneath His mighty hand
Please teach me to surrender that I might learn to stand
I know His love is teaching me to be a better man
One who walks by faith always trusting in His plan
I cannot even fathom what He's planning next for me
I will simply trust in Him until He lets me see
The future is important more so than yesterday
Though not nearly as important as the day I live today
I need to live each moment surrendered to His sovereign will
Till by His hand of grace my destiny I do fulfill
Let me not accomplish things through glory or through strife
With gentle words of wisdom let me always speak of life
With humble fear and trembling let me work my faith through You
Let not disputes or murmurings be found in what I do
I pray that I stay mindful and that in my heart I treasure
The work You're doing in me that my will is for Your pleasure
Wise as the fiercest serpent but harmless as the dove
Pour me out a brilliant flash of Your agape love

(Philippians 2:1-15)

"Motormouth"

I'm a motormouth yeah I admit it
When I get going it's hard to quit it
I'll talk and talk and talk all day
I guess I've got a lot to say
At least that's how I was before
But now I'm learning less is more
I used to be just blah blah blah
Yeah all day long just rah rah rah
I'm learning how to shut it down
Pump the brakes so folks don't drown
A well placed word that's said with care
And knowing why God placed me there
And when someone lends me their ear
I must make sure my words are clear
But knowing how to listen right
Brings every conversation light
One things for sure I am not shy
God made me this way He knows why
It's why He gives me every poem
If they can't hear I can show em
Just wanted you to know what's up
I've said enough so I'll just shut up

"MPH"

Listen up babygirl your birthday's today

I miss you so much and you're so far away

I know you miss us and you're probably mad

But we both love you honey your mom and your dad

We've had some rough times but things will get better

With God's hand to guide us we'll soon be together

They call you Annie but that's not your real name

People think it's from drugs but that is just lame

Mystical Purple is what we named you

I signed your birth certificate and put Hayes on it too

What your name means most can't understand

Honey that's cause it comes straight from God's hand

Your first name means reality of a spiritual kind

A deep inner light beyond what the senses can find

Your middle name's rare as far as names go

Someone else may have it but I don't think so

Air is transparent and water is too

But when seen all at once their color is blue

So blue is divine like the heavens of God

While red stands for earth also called sod

When they come together they form a fine hue

Majestic is purple and gorgeous like you

Your last name is Hayes like the mist in the distance

Though it's been changed your dad has persistence

Your name contains Love, Power and Beauty

And that really fits cause you're such a cutie

I used to live fast before I was knowing

Till you came along now you're the speed I am going

Yes the true name we gave you is light as a feather

It's the cloud that's stirred up when a life comes together

Yeah I miss you honey and Momma does too

We couldn't be there today so this poem's for you

Happy Birthday
Mystical Purple Hayes
Love Mom and Dad

"Mud Check"

Judge me O Lord search my whole heart

From Your narrow Way let me not part

For I trust in You and I shall not slide

Your Word it is true and so I abide

Examine me prove me try my heart's reins

Where I am soft send me life's pains

For I see Your kindness I walk in Your Truth

I've no time for haters looking for proof

I'm done with the wicked I'm sick of their ways

I've got better things to do with my days

Like shining Your Light and sharing Your Word

To all in the world who haven't yet heard

Cast me not Lord in the midst of the sinners

Give me a heart to be one of the winners

Cleanse me redeem me purge my complaints

And teach me to stand as one of Your Saints

"My Cry"

I cry to You Lord please hear my plea

Forsake me not Lord be not silent to me

Bind me not Lord like the wicked in chains

Make not my lot of their portion of pains

They lie to their neighbors with sweet words of peace

But of their wicked works there is no cease

They heed not Your Word nor the deeds of Your hands

They simply ignore Your sovereign commands

Blessed are You for You hear my cries

I trust in You Lord destroy all their lies

Lord You are my Strength and You are my Shield

By faith in Your Word my life has been healed

Gladly I go to the task You've appointed

For You are the Strength of all Your anointed

Fill me up Father with the hunger and thirst

To do only Your will and to put others first

(Psalm 28)

"My Flesh"

My flesh doth cry out it's lonely and torn

It aches to forsake all the vows that I've sworn

My flesh doth cry out it's battered and weak

With a tongue that blurts out what I should not speak

My flesh doth cry out it wants to be first

But when it's indulged it can't be reversed

My flesh is puffed up with lust and vain pride

Weary I am of this thorn in my side

My flesh has been cursed from cradle to grave

It won't make it through and I won't be its slave

My flesh is His temple where His Spirit dwells

Till He calls us home and we cast off these shells

My flesh it is tired yet still I push on

Please give me strength Lord to just carry on

My spirit is willing though my flesh it is weak

Please help me to listen and hear when You speak

This flesh is Your flesh these hands are Your hands

My honor and joy to obey Your commands

"My Gift from Heaven"

My gift from heaven she's soft and she's sweet

From the crown of her head to the soles of her feet

My gift from heaven she's safe and she's warm

She shelter's my heart from life's angry storm

My gift from heaven is goodness and light

And she fuels my heart to do what is right

My gift from heaven is perfectly fine

Her beauty grows daily the sweetest of wine

My gift from heaven is priceless and pure

For what ails my heart she is the cure

My gift from heaven she's simply the best

My prayer to You Lord that our love stands the test

Thank you my Father I know that she's true

For the love in her heart comes directly from You

"My God"

My God is awesome my God is strong
He gave me the words to write in this song
My God is holy my God is pure
His Word is unchanging steady and sure
My God is my refuge my God is my strength
His presence goes with me throughout the whole length
My God raised the mountains my God poured the seas
He brings down the mighty puts them on their knees
My God hung the heavens my God placed the stars
And He's written His lessons on each of my scars
My God is a Tower a Light in the dark
His arrows are sharp and they don't miss the mark
My God sends the rain my God stirs the wind
And He pricks my heart when I have sinned
My God is a Fortress My God is a Rock
The Head of the corner that first building Block
My God's on your lips in every last breath
When you can't say His Name then you have met death
My God made it all yes every last bit
My God is your God though you may not admit
My God shows great mercy my God is not lame
He's patiently waiting and calling your name
My God is the Answer my God is the Way
And He's built us a city where forever we'll stay

"My Part"

What has God revealed to me
That I am but a man
And though that may not seem like much
I'm part of His great plan
For I was born to do great things
This life is not a game
So armoured up and sanctified
I go forth in His Name
Along the way I get to see
A seed or two take take root
And when His face shines forth His grace
Right past the weeds they shoot
And so I will continue
To seek His face and pray
For those still lost I come across
That need to find their way
We go forth toward the harvest
And though we may be few
I know my Lord has brought me here
Because He always knew
That one day I would stand for Him
As He stood up for me
What shall I say "too hard the way"
He died to set me free!
So if I suffer for Him
What joy it brings my heart
To lead the way and in that day
Say Lord I've done my part
(Matthew 9:37,38)

"My Plea"

O Lord of heaven earth and sea

Let me learn humility

Cleanse my heart and make me humble

Lead me Lord so I don't stumble

Give to me an iron streak

And make my spirit strong and meek

Teach me patience to endure

Keep my purpose wholly pure

And though this world is dark and torn

Meet me early every morn

Scourge from me all thoughts of pride

Impart Your joy deep down inside

Let Your Spirit shine on me

To go and set the captives free

Bless me dress me send me out

With boldness let me sing and shout

Give me discernment and restraint

And send me forth an Iron Saint!

"My Sins"

My sins they were many my sins were too much

My sins dulled my mind till I was out of touch

My sins hurt my family my sins hurt my friends

My sins hurt my neighbors to achieve my own ends

My sins grieved the Spirit my sins fed my self

My sins stole my freedom set me on the shelf

My sins cost my children my sins cost my wife

My sins spun me out and screwed up my life

My sins they were wicked my sins were not fair

My sins were too heavy for this man to bear

My sins broke me down my sins brought me loss

My sins led me to that old rugged cross

My sins are forgiven my sins every one

My sins are washed clean by the Blood of the Son

"My Walk"

Can I get a moment Lord
We really need to talk
Your Spirit has revealed to me
Some missteps in my walk
Your still small voice convicts me Lord
And I need to heed Your call
For if I don't obey Your Word
I'm headed for a fall
My best laid plans are rubbish Lord
When I step outside Your will
I need You Holy Spirit
To simply come and fill
My thoughts and my emotions
Will lead me far astray
I need to stand upon Your Word
To guide me every day
Repentance means to turn from sin
To stand for what is right
Not lurking in the shadows
But right out in Your light
I'm asking You to teach me Lord
To be a better man
One who knows and shows Your love
A servant in Your plan
Thank You Lord for hearing me
I'm glad we had this talk
I need You so to help me grow
That in You I may walk!

"My Word"

My word means a lot whenever I give it
It's all that I've got so I need to live it
A man of my word is how I wish to be known
The truth that I speak is written in stone
Many these days simply lie to each other
But those aren't the type I want as my brother
My word is my bond that's how it should be
You know what you get when you talk to me
Some folks may not like what I have to say
But at least I don't change it day after day
What I say today I'll stand by tomorrow
And because I stand by it I won't have to borrow
A thought or a feeling or any weak thing
The truth that I speak has its very own ring
A promise from God through His Word shall be done
And my word is His seal that I am His son
I swear not by heaven I swear not by earth
Nor by my mother who gave me my birth
A gift from my Father with which He does bless
That my no would mean no and my yes would mean yes

"Needful"

Basically I'm broken
Torn by lust and pride
But thanks to Christ I have a hope
For this my Saviour died
I used to think I knew a thing
Or two about this walk
But flesh crept in and led to sin
And smashed me on The Rock
I thought I had the power
To live and serve my King
But lately He has shown me
That I know not a thing
Only by His mercy
His Love, His tender grace
Am I able to hold up my head
Or even show my face
Each day I am unlearning
The stuff I thought I knew
As I trust Christ who paid the price
That I should make it through
So what's the point I'm making
What do I have to say
That there's simply no mistaking
I need Jesus every day!
(Ephesians 2:8)

"New Year"

A bright and shiny new year is happening for me
Another calendar of gifts that God wants me to see
A fresh new batch of blessings that He is pouring out
And even when they're hard ones I really have no doubt
Seeing far beyond that than which we ever could
He's works all things together to give that which is good
He knows me and He shows me each and every day
His plans for me much better than I dare even say
He broadens my horizons He lights my path before
And gives me inspiration to boldly walk right through each door
I'm learning limitations are mostly self-imposed
And doors which God has opened no one has ever closed
In faith I must walk through them and not be stopped by doubt
I must believe and so receive that God will work it out
This year will be much better than any year before
Let each and every one to come show me so much more
More of God's great mercy His grace and boundless love
Let my heart and mind be set on that which is above
I'm grateful for the vision to see what He does show
As deep within my heart of hearts He lets me truly know
How deep how great how broad how wide how true that His love is
Assuring me forever more that I am truly His

"No More"

No more sin no more lies
No more selfish compromise
No more drama no more stress
No more making things a mess
No more trouble no more strife
No more screwing up my life
No more booze no more weed
No more life at breakneck speed
No more dealing no more meth
No more selling others death
No more greed no more junk
No more living like a punk
No more knives no more guns
No more suicidal runs
No more pipe no more point
No more time spent in the joint
No more come ups no more licks
No more hooking up with chicks
No more shoulda's no more maybe's
No more rippin off my babies
No more doubts no more fears
No more non-essential tears
No more pain no more bother
No more moves without my Father

"N.O.T.W."

The simple sound of silence
Tis not a sound at all
But rather is the absence of
Cacophany's strange call
The lights that light our cities
And help us find our way
Diminish how we see the stars
And stretch out every day
The constant stream of data
Information overload
The more we cram into our brains
No wonder men explode
There's very little downtime
Jacked up around the clock
And constantly some new idea
Someone's trying to hock
It seems that things are winding up
Much tighter every day
And those who choose to disagree
Are simply in the way
It's getting hard to tolerate
The mandates on my speech
Was this why grandpa spilled his blood
Upon some foreign beach
The devil wants us trippin
Like Nero thrashin Rome
But I have news for him my friends
This world is not my home!

"O' Lord"

Love me Holy Father
Draw me to Your Son
Adopt me to Your family so
We all may be as One
Captivate my soul O' Lord
Bind my heart to You
Give to me discerning light
Show me what to do
Fill me Holy Spirit
Until I overflow
Give to me a tongue to teach
That others too may know
Search my heart and soul O' Lord
Look me through and through
Purge me from the wickedness
That turns away from You
Finally Lord I have one thing
That I would ask of Thee
O' wretched sinner that I am
Be merciful to me
(Luke 18:13)

"Old Glory"

Is this the land of the free
And the home of the brave
What, free to scorn God
And the blessings He gave
Where is our honor
Our national pride
Has the American spirit
Shriveled and died
Is our country so twisted
And so far off course
That we can't find our way
Back to the Source
We need to get up
And shake off the dust
And get back to basics
Like "In God We Trust"
Come on my Brothers
And my Sisters too
Stand up for the Lord
And the red, white and blue
"God Bless America"

"Pain"

Pain is God's great warning system
That keeps us from great harm
A little taste of "that's not good"
Which raises the alarm
A note to pay attention
To put some focus there
So we don't neglect those things
Which do require care
Now you can stub your toe you know
And wow how that does smart
But I'd gladly stub a thousand toes
To spare a broken heart
Much pain is self inflicted
From choices that we make
But sometimes there is pain and yet
We made not one mistake
Only God can understand
His plans for you and me
And really it is just too much
For our little minds to see
Even there in heaven
There's pain in God's own heart
It says that He's longsuffering
That all should not depart
So next time when you're suffering
Just know He suffers too
And thank Him for the grace He gives
That more could make it through
(2 Peter 3:9)

"Passover"

Long long ago in a far distant land
The Lord spoke to Moses and gave a command
On this first month and on the tenth day
Each house takes a lamb and brings it to stay
Unblemished and perfect the best price ye shall pay it
Then on the fourteenth ye shall take it and slay it
Take of its blood and paint every door
On the outside as a sign to the Lord
For I come to smite the first born of the land
But where I see blood I will hold back My hand
Roast the Lamb's flesh and eat the whole thing
Serve unleavened bread and bitter herbs bring
Keep your shoes on with your staff in your hand
Get ready to move as I smite the whole land
You shall keep this day to the Lord as a feast
And tell how I killed their firstborn man and beast
Tell each generation tell every last one
How I passed over you and killed Pharaoh's son
This picture tells how we are spared from the pain
When our sins are washed clean by the Lamb that was slain

"Pattern"

I got some bitter news today
My eldest son has gone astray
My sin has left a crimson stain
And caused my family so much pain
My selfish ways have left a rift
I dropped the ball and let things drift
The devil has my oldest son
Strung out on his heroin
The devil's plan to cause me fear
But I trust God to see him clear
I hope and pray Lord hear my pleas
Please put Jesse on his knees
Use this sickness and this strife
To draw him to Your gift of life
Let his sorrow and his loss
Draw him broken to Your cross
Keep him Father with Your care
Send Your warring angels there
Bring him Jesus to your fold
Prove him Father solid gold
All these years I have denied
The pools of tears my father cried
I know now what I have done
To my father through my son
For now I'm in my father's place
As tears run down and stain my face
But pain is what completes the man
My faith is Yours I trust Your plan
To break and heal and teach my boy
To fill his heart with love and joy
That only comes from knowing You
But oh the pain we must go through
Heal him Father set him free
Then please God send him back to me

"Peace"

As bombs go off in public
And bullets scar our schools
We're set upon on every side
By cowards and by fools
No logic to their madness
They're demonically possessed
Fear cannot be our answer
As we're put to the test
D.C. ain't got the answers
This stuff's just getting worse
They cannot change men's hearts and minds
Or keep a balanced purse
They jump and shout and say lookout
They always have a word
But what about the unborn cry
That's never ever heard
We want to pick and choose what's sin
Who should or not be killed
But last time that I checked my friend
That job's already filled
The devil and his minions
Their plan is to distract
Get you to lose your focus
So you can be attacked
Saint Peter walked on water
I tell you JESUS SAVES
So keep your vision fixed on Him
Not on the crashing waves
Prayer is what is needed
Each and every day
The peace that comes from knowing Christ
He is the only Way!

"Plugged In"

Tenacity in action
Hold a steady course
Drawing satisfaction
Straight up from the Source
Like poetry in motion
His plans for you unfold
New mercies each and every day
Never getting old
Boot straps buckled
Grip white knuckled
Sounds good but it's flawed
Batteries run down my friend
So get plugged in to God
Each valley has a reason
So too each shining peak
The light He bathes you in up there
Reminds you when you're weak
That through Christ you can do all things
When times are dark and bleak
It matters not just what you think
Nor even how you feel
Those things will change and rearrange
God's Word will seal the deal
So count your blessings every one
The great and yes the small
For each was caused by God my friend
He sent them one and all

"Pneumatikos"

Born of water born of blood

Born of the Spirit from above

Not of flesh nor of man

But all according to God's plan

You hear the wind when it blows

From whence it cometh nobody knows

Our teacher comes on the wings of a dove

And gives us truth to speak in love

He gives us power over the flesh

To leave it all and start out fresh

By things of death we are sickened

But by His breath we are quickened

So cleanse your heart refuse to sin

Just open up and ask Him in

(John 3:3,5-8)

"Praise"

Unto Thee O my Lord do I lift up my soul
To be one with You that is my goal
O my Lord and my God in Thee do trust I
Regardless of all even though I may die
Where I place my faith only You have I named
Keep me my Father let me not be ashamed
Let not my foes win out over me
In all of my triumphs I will glorify Thee
Let none of Your Saints be saddled with shame
But let the transgressors quake at Your Name
Teach me Thy paths Lord show me Thy ways
Teach me to laugh and lengthen my days
Lead me in truth and sanctify me
For You are my Saviour in You I am free
Your love and Your mercies are finer than gold
Transcending our lives from beyond days of old
Cast far from Thee my sins and transgressions
Have mercy on me when I make my confessions
Condemn me not Lord for every mistake
Remember me Lord for Thy goodness sake

"Prayer"

Prayer in the morning prayer late at night

Prayer without ceasing through the daylight

Prayer at the table when we sit down

Prayer for our nation and prayer for our town

Prayer for our brothers prayer for their wives

Prayer for our children throughout their whole lives

Prayer when we're grateful prayer when we're sad

Prayer for forgiveness when we've done bad

Prayer for assistance prayer for God's hand

Prayer for His wisdom so we can understand

Prayer when we're lonely prayer when we're scared

Prayer done while planning so that we are prepared

Prayer for God's guidance prayer for His will

Prayer for His Spirit to come in and fill

Prayer to the Father prayer through the Son

Prayer of all prayers that we all may be One

"Preach"

Unctuous elocution inspires me to write

So possibly some may just see a tiny bit of light

God's awesome love surrounds us of that there is no doubt

Some need to hear it whispered while some require a shout

Countless are the methods our Father does employ

When guiding men to wisdom and filling them with joy

There's power in the spoken word and in those written well

The Gospel's call is free to all to save their souls from hell

It's really hard to fathom why any would reject

The awesome privilege to be known as one of God's elect

Though this world's been entered God's light come pouring in

Still men love the darkness enslaved by their own sin

And even though that darkness spreads further every day

I must not stop contending nor change that which I say

While political correctness bids me to compromise

It's flawed in its own premise a tangled web of lies

So I'll just keep on preaching that old school Gospel call

To fast and wild or meek and mild 'tis offered free to all

Keep marching on my brethren through fire or frost or flood

Trumpeting the message of Christ's redeeming Blood!

"Presence"

In the presence of the Lord
My joy is truly full
To spend each moment with Him
Despite the constant pull
The world with all its issues
The sin the lies the noise
Has no effect upon me
When my spirit He employs
But I must focus on Him
Not only when in prayer
But share each moment with Him
For He's with me everywhere
A constant conversation
With my sovereign King
For He is always with me
Sharing everything
And like we seek attention
When talking with a friend
Let me not forget Him
Lest I should offend
His presence is a comfort
A light that leads me on
And gives me full assurance
That I can carry on

"Prince of Peace"

And what would be my purpose
Were I not on The Way
Would I have hope to help me cope
To hold against that day
Or would my life be motions
Just things that I went through
Some of this to get me that
Or stuff that I could do
Just things to keep me busy
Or keep me well amused
Even things that are not bad
Until they are abused
Or would my mind be burdened
With worry and with stress
As I attempted to make sense
Of life's chaotic mess
Or maybe I'd be angry
Cause things don't go my way
Unable to see reason
No matter what you say
There's no rest for the wicked
In spite of all we do
Without the Son of God my friend
We will not make it through
Through the endless thicket
Where thorns will never cease
Until we trust in Christ alone
The perfect Prince of Peace

"Promises"

Lend me your ear as I tell you a tale
Of pain and confusion and time spent in jail
Of hustlers and hookers and hoodlums and thugs
Of twisted meth cookers and all kinds of drugs
Of criminal schemes and selfish desires
Which shatter our dreams and turn us to liars
Of promises made and words that were spoken
Eventually though they all just got broken
Our kids left behind and maybe a wife
While we rot in jail and miss their whole life
Them out in the world and us behind bars
The time spent without us is sure to leave scars
Those kids need their dad and their mom needs her man
To raise them together now that was God's plan
I've tried and I've tried I just seem to keep falling
I can't do it alone so to You Lord I'm calling
With shame in my heart and tears on my face
I come humbly Lord to Your throne of grace
I'm sick of my "self" I don't wanna be bad
Come fill me up Lord so I can be a good dad

(Hebrews 4:16)

"Pure Religion"

Count it joy when tempted
Patience your reward
When your faith is tried and still
You wait upon The Lord
If you lack in wisdom
Ask ye shall receive
The greatest gifts He showers on
Them that do believe
If any man among you
Is tempted by his lust
Remember that all sin breeds death
A promise you should trust
So let each man be swift to hear
But slow to speech or wrath
Let him first consider that
Which keeps him on God's path
Many are the hearers
But doers far between
Those that walk their faith for real
Know just what I mean
We know that pure religion
Is true in word and deed
It keeps itself unspotted
And gives to those in need
There are no perfect people
For all men make mistakes
But those who practice what they preach
May have just what it takes

(James 1:2-27)

"Purpose"

To live without a purpose
Is not to live at all
Yeah living large and taking charge
Is really thinking small
Our tiny minds can't fathom
What's dearest to God's heart
Not building of cathedrals
But doing just our part
A simple act of kindness
Or maybe just a smile
And yet it may take sacrifice
Like Simon's bloody mile
I know that people come and go
That money can't buy love
And though a toy may bring me joy
My peace comes from above
So when I hear God's whisper
Deep down in my heart
It's solely up to me to stand
And humbly do my part
Some say purpose driven
I choose Spirit led
The meat of sharing God's great grace
My sweetest daily bread

(John 4:34)

"Questions"

Are you washed in the Blood
'Neath the ever cleansing flood
Have you been to the Cross are you clean
Have you been on your knees
Has He ever heard your pleas
Or do you even know what I mean
Have you broke down and wept
Has your heart's floor been swept
Did you feel sweet release when you cried
Does it mean that much to you
What our Saviour did go through
When He laid down His life and He died
Is this all that there is
Or do you know that you're His
And that you are the apple of His eye
Are you sure you'll be there
When we meet Him in the air
Are you sealed in your spirit can you fly
Do you know you will see
When this life it sets you free
Will you finally be home when you die

"Rain Song"

A long time ago before the world had seen rain
The actions of men brought God nothing but pain
Their hearts were so wicked and their thinking so bent
That He'd ever made man the Lord's heart did repent
Since the whole world was evil and completely insane
He decided to cleanse it and wash it with rain
But there was a man who'd found grace in His eyes
He did what was right and he never told lies
Tenth son from Adam of all men the best
Noah in Hebrew means comfort or rest
The Lord spoke to Noah said listen to Me
All flesh will I end by raising the sea
Listen up now to what I will say
Through faith in My Word you will find a way
If you do all the things that I tell you to do
You and your family will all make it through
Make thee an ark of long gopher wood beams
Within and without spread pitch on the seams
Make it so wide so tall and so long
Do this precisely so it will be strong
Thou shalt make a window one cubit's length wide
A door thou shalt fashion and set in the side
Then God said to Noah behold I even I

Do bring forth a flood that all flesh may die
But a covenant with you I will employ
You and your family I will not destroy
And you shall take with you of each type of flesh
A pair of each kind so they can start again fresh
Ye shall make a great store of food and all seeds
To sow them one day and see to your needs
Each one of these things in faith did he do
For he knew in his heart what God spoke was true
When it started to rain he was six hundred years old
He was wise in his years doing all he was told
So the animals came and by pairs did they board
Of course they were each led that way by the Lord
Then Noah went in with his sons and their wives
This was the soul passage to salvage their lives
Those eight precious souls and the beasts on each floor
Once all were in place God sealed up the door
The windows of heaven gave forth a great shower
As the fountains down deep broke up with God's power
The people looked up at the rain falling down
As the waters prevailed and they started to drown
Yes it rained and it rained for the next forty days
And for five months thereafter it continued to raise
Higher and higher would this flood ever stop
Not till it covered the last mountain top

Now all flesh was dead upon the whole earth
Of fowl man and cattle and all that gave birth
Yes every last thing off that ark had met death
All those whose nostrils had tasted life's breath
Then after those months as they waited and waited
God closed the fountains and the waters abated
For seven long months and seventeen days
They'd floated and floated on endless gray waves
Until the tenth month when the waters did drop
That's when they saw the first mountain top
Then Noah sent forth a raven and dove
To search for dry land from the air up above
When the dove came back tired he waited a week
This time she came back with a leaf in her beak
So he waited a week and sent her back out
When she did not return then he had no doubt
He took off the ark's cover and he looked around
And what he saw there was the face of the ground
On Mount Ararat is where they had arrived
Because of his faith the whole family survived
Then God said to Noah go forth from the ark
So he built Him an altar and gave it a spark
Of every clean beast he sent forth a sweet savour
Giving thanks to the Lord for His mercy and favour
When God smelled that smell He said in His heart

I'll curse not the ground anymore for man's part
Neither will I bring an end to all things
Due to the evil man's heart surely brings
While this earth remains God is the reason
Day follows night and we have every season
God blessed Noah then and gave to him all
The beasts of the earth from the great to the small
If it moves ye may have it and take it for meat
And all the green herbs of the ground you may eat
But touch not the blood and kill not your brother
Or your life I'll require at the hands of another
Go forth and be fruitful and bring forth great life
You and your sons each one with his wife
Shem Ham and Japeth these were his sons
The nations of man would descend from these ones
Then God made a promise and gave us a sign
Way up in the heavens line upon line
So next time you look at the clouds in the sky
Remember His promise for God does not lie
He won't end all life with a flood He said no
And this is the reason He gave us His bow
(Genesis Chapters 6 – 9)

"Rapture"

Now you might think you know the way

But I am looking to that day

When trumpet sounds and bodies rise

To meet the Son amidst the skies

And at that point I'll rise as well

As He perfects this mortal shell

Snatched right off this broken world

To see His glory there unfurled

For death has lost its wicked sting

The grave could not contain my King

Regardless what the whole world gives

It matters not my Saviour lives

The life He has He wants to share

That all may rise and meet Him there

Till that day I watch and wait

And trust Christ to secure my fate

(1Corinthians 15:50-58)

"Rat Race"

Inconsistent algorithms running through my brain
Lost in thought and so distraught distractions from my pain
A world of domination supply demand and feed
A hopeless situation just work and sleep and breed
Over-thinking everything I need to understand
Am I a cosmic accident or was this all pre-planned
My mind says I must see the proof
Though Truth's already penned
If I require a sign from God my brain is not my friend
But maybe if I ask Him to reveal Himself He will
Or should I keep that to myself I might just need a pill
Or maybe I should buy some clothes a car a truck a bike
Or maybe I should take a trip to someplace I might like
What if I climbed a mountain or sailed across the sea
Or set up some appointment some place I had to be
But maybe there is more to life than that which meets the eye
A purpose for each step I take and only God knows why
And maybe that's the reason I never have enough
To really keep me happy 'cause hey it's only stuff
It seems to me what's best is free at least I'm learning now
And so I pray each night and day that God will show me how
To be a better father a brother son or friend
Who brings a better message than that the world does send
So hopefully this helps you see the one way you can win it
To beat the rat race of the world quite simply don't get in it!

"Real Men"

Real men are what's needed
Real men are a must
Real men keep their word
And that you can trust
Real men are called Daddy
Real men stick around
Real men know what's right
And they will stand their ground
Real men are not perfect
Real men face their fears
Real men aren't ashamed
When they shed tears
Real men need each other
Real men know the score
Real men know what God
Gave them brothers for
Real men are a blessing
Real men say their prayers
Real men trust the Lord
For they know that He cares

"Receive"

Acceptance of God's will for me
And peace with what that is
Gratitude for all He does
The proof that I am His
The willingness to walk with Him
No matter where we go
A life that glorifies His Name
So others too may know
Now I could whine and cry around
Bout' stuff that I ain't got
Or I can claim the blessing
And receive what I am taught
Yes I could simply pine away
On what my heart longs for
Or I can seek my Saviour's face
To know Him more and more
Now to the world it may just seem
His will is not that fair
But we will count this all chump change
When we meet Him in the air
The toughest part of life my friend
The first one hundred years
Then better days which will amaze
When Jesus wipes our tears

"Redeemed"

Redeemed from my transgressions
Spared eternal flame
Due to Jesus sacrifice
The Father knows my name
Saved from my own wickedness
Not for the works I've done
I'd made a mess of me for sure
And still God sent His Son
The noblest thing I've ever done
Tis nothing when compared
To what my Master did that day
That my soul might be spared
He came here just for me you know
I tell you this is true
But know this in your heart my friend
He also came for you
What a priceless gift we have
To know Him and be known
Adopted to His family
And called by Him His own
And when I dwell upon it
The tears well up in me
I can't explain my spirit's gain
Since Jesus set me free

"Refining Fire"

Inconceivability yeah that's been covered to
Countless preparations made
That you could make it through
No eye hath seen no ear hath heard
Nor heart been entered in
With all the cares the Father has completely sown within
His sanctifying presence dwells richly in your soul
Prompting your ascension till in Him you're made whole
A never ending process divinely pre-designed
Consuming fire that He is leaving us refined
Impurities are not burned up when heated to lukewarm
But hotter than the sun the bolts He sends within the storm
It's hard to see His purpose in all that we go through
But coming out the other side we can't deny it's true
We've grown a little stronger and wisdom has increased
When touched by His adversity potential is released
Our failures His reminders lest we should forget
No matter how improved we are He's still not finished yet
So patient with our progress of that there is no doubt
His plans prevail they will not fail yes He will work it out
He's teaching us we're built to last and nothing ever made
Can separate us from His love or beat the price He paid
He's taken all our burdens replaced each heart of stone
And proven in a thousand ways that we are not alone
Most precious to the Father are His darling little ones
His Spirit bearing witness that He now calls us sons

"Reflecting"

Sitting here reflecting on
The things I get to see
Each and every day a gift
Since Jesus set me free
No more chains and shackles
No strongholds in my brain
The Truth has set me free at last
He's vanquished all that pain
Instead of stress and worry
I gaze upon His face
At times I'm simply speechless
Reflecting on His grace
As pen describes on paper
The things I think and feel
He's etched upon my heart His love
And nothing is more real
To know Him is to show Him
Each and every day
To shine His light and do what's right
All along the way
Yes sitting here reflecting
Brings such peace to me
So slow your roll and calm your soul
Let Jesus set you free

"Reflections"

Hear me O Shepherd of Israel's flock
Plant my feet firmly upon solid Rock
Let Your glory blaze Shekinah shine forth
To the south east and west from the sides of the north
Stir up Thy strength come now and save us
Teach us to walk in the grace that You gave us
Most High Lord of hosts show us the Way
Order our steps day after day
Turn us again come show us Your face
Remind every one Who created this place
Quicken us Lord so we call upon You
Set straight our course so we can make it through
Uphold us and keep us with Your mighty hand
Strengthen us Lord in Your might let us stand
Flow through our spirits and make our hearts true
Make each Saint to shine a reflection of You

"Relapse"

We just don't kick our wounded no that's not what we do
We help them up and dust them off
To help them make it through
Progress not perfection as long as there's desire
The will to just continue is all that we require
Now some will take advantage they think this is a game
And if that is their state of mind that's really pretty lame
Some people just want help with what they want to do
That's not the kind of help they need they're only using you
But if they're really willing to do just what it takes
Then grace is what is called for when they make mistakes
It's natural to get angry that happens when we care
Most of all when we get hurt by those with whom we share
Our love and friendship freely that's why it hurts so much
The ones we let inside our hearts have purchase there to touch
It's gonna freakin happen not always but it does
Yet still we must continue yes we need to just because
To keep what we've been given and by its power grow
We've got to give that stuff away and let it through us flow
We've got to trust the process for God will work things out
And we must all accept that fact without one single doubt
The best thing we can do for them on any given day
Shine His light do what's right and don't forget to pray

"Relax"

The defects in my character
Are very plain to see
Very plain to everyone
Everyone but me
But lately I have done some work
And in that process found
That many of my tactics are
Not so very sound
In looking at the way I walk
And talk and treat my friends
I'm seeing I do damage there
So I must make amends
At times I'm overbearing
Sometimes just downright rude
That's not my intention
Don't want to be that dude
I'm working on relaxing
Not being so intense
At putting others feelings first
Avoiding all offense
For having all the answers
Does not a man make wise
But seeing others points of view
And finding compromise
I know things will work out now
That none will need pretend
When taking stock of people
They'll count me as a friend

"Rest"

A psalm a hymn a spiritual song
That beats in my heart all the day long
The dreams that I have deep in the night
Faith from just knowing all will be right
The smile that's staked a claim on my face
And knowing that every last thing has a place
Trusting the Lord to be right on time
And give me each word to perfectly rhyme
Not rushing in like a fool that's half-cocked
And knowing for sure that my destiny's locked
Contentment with nothing to hold in my hands
The freedom from worldly possessions demands
Not having to deal with the stress or the worry
And oh what a blessing not to be in a hurry
Not constantly trippin and watching the clock
That stuff doesn't matter when you stand on the Rock
I can't be made happy with some stupid toy
Not now that I've tasted of genuine joy
I've no time for rubbish I'll stay with the Best
My heart's been made whole for I've entered Christ's rest

"Reveille"

The calling of the Brethren
The assembling of the Saints
A standard's being raised
That transcends the world's restraints
The Voice that lit the stars
And poured the raging sea
Is summoning His children
And whispering to me
The rulers of the darkness
And powers that confuse
Are contesting every inch
Cause they know they're going to lose
I see the Master's hand
And I'm learning every day
To recognize the Saints
That I meet along the way
I'm standing and I'm waiting
And sharpening my sword
I'm standing on the Word
And I'm waiting on the Lord
(Isaiah 40:31)

"Salvation"

Salvation is a three part deal
For this my Saviour bruised His heel
Upon the cross He took my place
And covered me in boundless grace
He plunged me 'neath the cleansing flood
And washed me in His precious Blood
Because He took my place and died
My debt is paid I'm justified
And since He paid that debt for me
I'm free from sin's foul penalty
But that's not all no He's not through
That's part one now here's part two
He's put His Spirit into me
To strengthen me and set me free
I'm shedding things like lust and pride
Through Him I'm being sanctified
Yes day by day and hour by hour
I'm overcoming sin's dark power
That's two so far now one to go
But till Christ comes that's all we'll know
For when we rise with those who've died
It's then that we'll be glorified
And once we're filled with Jesus' essence
Then we'll be free from sin's foul presence
No pain no death no sickness there
When we meet Christ up in the air
How beautiful how pure how sweet
Once our salvation is complete

"School Days"

Can you tell me why a tree is green
And what do all these flowers mean
Why are the mountains tall and proud
And what about that puffy cloud
Can you explain the rocks and sand
And waves we see at edge of land
How about the stars and moon
Or the sun that shines above at noon
The ice that goes for miles and miles
Or the snow that falls and lands in piles
And what about the little birds
And all the beasts that run in herds
The spookiness of thick white fog
Or the happiness of a puppy dog
Can you help me to understand
The comfort of a helping hand
Or how about the reason why
We hate to see a loved one die
The beauty and the pain we know
Is meant to help us learn and grow
Thank You Lord for being cool
And giving us this awesome school

"Seeking"

Endless applications
Distractions to be sure
A never ending quest to find
Something that will cure
That little tear deep down inside
The itch that can't be scratched
There is no person place or thing
Nor plan that can be hatched
There is no foreign substance
To change the way we feel
It's all a lie to make you die
To numb you from what's real
External application lacks
The power to refresh
There's no real joy in any toy
Or feeding of the flesh
And he that builds an empire
Sand castles in the sky
How much better to receive
A mansion when we die
Plus all this stuff just makes it tough
And simply does confuse
It blinds your eyes to jeopardize
The gift you should not lose
So focus in that you may win
The one good thing that's true
Seek God's kingdom first my friend
And He shall add to you
(Matthew 6:33)

"Send Me"

Humbly I kneel before Your throne of grace
As seraphim burn and cover their face
Holy and holy and holy once more
The sound of the praise rattles the door
Woe is me Lord for I am undone
Wash me O Lord in the Blood of Your Son
O fiery angel bring me that coal
To lay on my mouth and heal my torn soul
Send me O Lord across the whole land
Proclaiming Your Word though they don't understand
Though from You they've turned
Please make clear the choice
I vow to go forth just give me Your voice
Please make smooth my path
And give me Your strength
Make my will Your own let me go the whole length
Please give me the strength to finish this cup
Though I'm fully aware how Your prophets end up
All I am asking let me do my part
Till then I will wait till You tell me to start

(Isaiah 6)

"Sent"

A heart to start and do my part

My Sword a course an iron horse

Your hand to guide and lead my ride

I go You lead if need I bleed

No fear no doubt Lord pour me out

Your patch to fly I-Den-Ti-Fy

A heart and scars to reach through bars

From You a plan to touch each man

A valid point to bring each joint

Your Bread I break my thirst You slake

You fill me up Your Word my cup

Free me Lord from sin's foul taint

And mount me up an Iron Saint

I gladly break the Bread You give

I Live to Read and Read to Live!

"Shadow"

Upon the billows tempest tossed
Chaos rules while we are lost
Nothing seems to go our way
How wicked are the games we play
Deeper down we dig the holes
At the peril of our souls
What we chase we cannot find
He is there but we are blind
Through our pain our strife our woes
He is there He always knows
The deepest darkest things we hide
And still He's there right by our side
All He does is right and true
It is done to strengthen you
You can bend or you can break
The choice is simply yours to make
On your feet or on your knees
He will hear your heartfelt pleas
Come now children to His throne
For we are His let that be known
This world must count as naught but loss
Come now Saints pick up your cross

"Share"

God shall not be mocked my friends
So be ye not deceived
As each man sows he too shall reap
Rewards shall be received
Just rewards may be quite good
But sometimes they are not
As he that soweth to his flesh
Shall of corruption rot
But he that sows to spirit
Shall of the Spirit yield
Everlasting life in Christ
And from death's stroke be healed
So let us not grow weary now
In doing all that's good
And let us pray to recognize
Exactly how we should
Walk in Christ-like meekness
This narrow rocky way
That all would have respect for us
And value what we say
Yes let us do to every man
As we'd be by them done
And let us have the courage now
To share with them God's Son
(Galatians 6)

"Silence"

There is a thing that's hard to find
But with it you can clear your mind
Yes silence is a fleeting thing
With all the noise this world does bring
The cars the phones the T.V. sets
The endless groans of screaming jets
It seems the world just won't slow down
In chaos it will surely drown
But if you plan and early rise
You may find a sweet surprise
If you can find a private place
And spend some time upon your face
Before your senses are assaulted
A time when He can be exalted
Our Lord will come and meet you there
With great and mighty things to share
Yes silence is a golden thing
Where one can hear the angel's wing
So take some time before the noise
To come and hear that still small voice

(Proverbs 8:17 & Jeremiah 33:3)

"Simmer Down"

When walking on the waters right through the crashing waves
The only light that keeps me right the fact that Jesus saves
Please give me single vision that I may make it through
Let all concerns and cares I have be wholly cast on You
Let every earthly friction and crisis that ensues
Be covered by Your love and grace and cast beneath my shoes
Please give me peace and wisdom to learn each lesson well
Reign in my hot emotions let not my anger swell
Let not my circumstances dictate my state of mind
Please keep me meek and humble and let my words be kind
I need You more than ever Lord I need to claim Your peace
I pray that You will fill my heart may Your love never cease
Please let it flow right through me please let my fears be gone
Please let Your perfect love cast out all fear that's going on
I pray for godly balance I pray that You will speak
Into the hearts and minds of all who lie and steal and sneak
I ask You Holy Spirit to completely overwhelm
Let every wicked spirit be cast out now from this realm
Please banish now the discord being sown within the ranks
I ask these things in confidence and so I give You thanks
I know that through the process I'm being made a better man
And knowing's half the battle when submitting to Your plan
Let no bridges be burnt down Lord but rather let them heal
But most of all I thank You Lord because You are so real
These days I'm seeing instantly the answers when I pray
And knowing that You're showing me You are the Only Way!

"Sin"

The soul that sinneth it shall die
The Word of God has told us why
When we sin we miss the mark
Instead of light it leads to dark
The devil tries to lead astray
And if we go we disobey
For we are told not to rebel
To dwell in sin will lead to hell
Death is the wages that are given for it
Its strength is the law but many ignore it
Not only is sin the wrong that we do
But not doing what's right that is sin too
Sins evil and twisted perverted and bent
The purpose behind it is not what God meant
For He brings abundance He wants us to win
But that simply won't happen when we choose to sin
Our Father is eager and willing to bless
But He will not do so when we transgress
All men are sinners and each one must choose
To claim Christ as Saviour or bear his own bruise
All sins are forgiven when washed in His Blood
So be a good sheep and shake off the mud
Don't wallow around like a swine in the mire
Or forever you'll burn in eternal hell-fire!

"Sisters"

My sisters mean so much to me
They always have for I can see
Reflections of my Father's love
Flowing down from high above
Down through them and onto me
They shine His light for all to see
Most of them are awesome mothers
Always caring for the brothers
And when my spirit needs a lift
I thank my Father for His gift
A sister is an awesome thing
The love they have they freely bring
Some are blood and some are more
The ones who are they know the score
Grow me Father strong and true
A brother they can look up to
My sisters they are precious pearls
Thank You Father for Your girls

"Sojourn"

Too soon old too late smart

But just in time to do our part

The pains we've known the scars we bear

They've taught us lessons we should share

If we'd slow down and help each other

Just walk it out a solid brother

How much more an awesome thing

To love and care and please my King

To spend myself in service here

Not holding life in this place dear

For we are merely passing through

There's nothing here for me or you

So seek ye first His kingdom friend

Walk by faith right till the end

And when your days on earth are done

You'll finally get to meet the Son

"Sons"

Sons of the mothers of the brothers of the sons
Only the Lord can number these ones
These ones were chosen long before birth
Even before the founding of earth
Their course is predestined their purpose is set
They are the Lord's though they may not know yet
A man of this type is often confused
Not yet understanding how he is to be used
One things for sure throughout his whole life
Every wrong step's brought him nothing but strife
The things of this world the lust and the pride
Give him a sick feeling deep down inside
He can't seem to fit in things aren't quite right
For he was designed to walk in God's light
His purpose in life must be achieved
He finds no contentment with the deceived
Then finally one day God's Spirit comes in
And gives him discernment to recognize sin
He's no longer blind and on the wrong course
When planning his steps he follows the Source
He now understands what it means to be free
And stand as the man God intends him to be

(Ephesians 6:10-20)

"Sovereign"

Destiny calls and so I must write
To glorify God while reflecting His light
The thoughts that I have the things that I see
Discerning His hand O what majesty
Miraculous blessings surrounding us all
No problem too big no matter too small
Sovereign provision and sustenance too
And sweet daily bread for me and for you
Wisdom to guide us found in His Word
His Spirit unlocking the things that we've heard
While deep in our hearts on tablets of flesh
He's written His love to each of us fresh
Not carved on some stone but down in our guts
For sharp is His Word and deeply it cuts
There's no need to ponder or take a long time
You know what is right and what is a crime
Believing is good for that's how we grow
But what a relief to finally know
To know that my Saviour my Master my King
Has everything covered yes every last thing

"Sow Seed"

Thou believest there is one God
I say thou doest well
The devils also know He's true
Yet still they'll burn in hell
What doth it profit brethren
To name Christ with your mouth
But when there's work to do up north
You're always headed south
I say that faith without works
Is deader than dry fish
And things don't get accomplished
While you simply sit and wish
And what good is a body
That's spirit has gone cold
It don't take long to know it's wrong
When it starts to mold
Now I won't tell you how to go
About the business of
Spreading forth the message
Of God's redeeming love
Don't do this just to please Him
He could not love you more
Go and serve Him just because
It's what He saved you for
To go forth and proclaim Him
To pray for those in need
Just sow in faith and trust that He
Will water every seed

"Stand"

The place where God has put you at
Is where you need to go to bat
Seize the day and do your best
To stand for Him and pass the test
The things that really rub you wrong
Are meant to build you true and strong
First of all there's no retreat
For that's accepting a defeat
Avoidance merely let's thing stew
And what's that really teaching you
Prayer is needed first of all
For every problem large or small
Next you need to start out fresh
Heed the Spirit not the flesh
Love will solve it don't use pride
His Word is where you must abide
Be patient meek and don't offend
God may reward you with a friend
Finally once you've done your part
Just ask the Lord to touch that heart

"Standing"

I'm standing on the promise
That God has set me free
Free to claim His Holy Name
And be who I should be
Not caught up in some battle
To try and prove I'm right
I'm really here to represent
And shine a little light
My life paints quite a picture
With all that I've been through
A brilliant demonstration
Of what God's love can do
It's hard to even fathom
The depths to which I went
Or how much it cost the Father
When to the world His Son was sent
I pray that I'm found worthy
Simply on my faith alone
That when I stand before Him
Through Christ my name is known
Yes I'm standing on the promise
That in Him there's no lack
And when this world has run its course
My Saviour's coming back

"Stars Above"

They say he drowned out in the pool
Yeah Brian Jones was pretty cool
Next we heard move over Rover
And just like that Jimi's trip was over
Then Janis went and split the scene
Too much down had claimed the queen
Jim Morrison just up and died
Broke on through to the other side
Duane Allman that swingin drinkin fighter
They finally caught that midnight rider
Then Ronnie left us without a word
At least he left to us Freebird
Next thing you know we lost Keith Moon
Who Are You his final tune
And then we lost ol' Moby Dick
When Bonzo left us we all felt sick
And just like that Bon was gone
Guess he felt like ridin on
Then shots were heard in New York City
When Lennon died it was such a pity
Then over the mountains and across the sky
When Randy flew we wondered why
And right when we felt we might stop hurtin
Just like Randy we lost Cliff Burton
And now just the other day
An air crash got ol' Stevie Ray
They may be gone though not forgotten
For them to go was really rotten
They gave us their music we gave them our love
So please God bless our stars above

"Sticks and Stones"

Sticks and stones may break my bones

And words may hurt as well

But deep inside I'm justified

My soul's been saved from hell

The power in the cross my friend

Will overcome your sin

Our Saviour paid the price that day

In Him we always win

Don't trust in man's devices

They always lead astray

By grace through faith trust Christ instead

HE IS THE ONLY WAY!

(John 14:6)

"Stirred Up"

Out of the darkness and into the light

No longer blind nor walking by sight

He that hath ears let him now hear

Your voice in his heart drawing him near

Near to the Cross drawn to his knees

With a heart of remorse lips uttering pleas

Let mercy and grace wash over his soul

To mend his torn spirit and raise him up whole

Stir up within him the grit and the nerve

To stand up for Christ and humbly go serve

Father please give him the vision and strength

To maintain Your course and go the whole length

Yes stir up his spirit and capture his heart

To put Your will first and just do his part

"Strength"

O Lord my Rock unto Thee will I cry

Forsake me not Lord lest I sicken and die

Hold not back Thy voice whisper to me

You are my choice for You set me free

Hear now my prayers as I cry unto Thee

My hands lifted up down on bended knee

Draw me not down with the wicked and lost

Their lips claim Your peace but their heart's full of frost

Your love they have not for Your Word they've ignored

They've simply no time for the works of the Lord

But blessed are You for You hear my cry

You've quickened me now so that I will not die

Lord You are my Strength and You are my Shield

In You I abide for my spirit You've sealed

Yes You are the Strength of all Your anointed

You lift us up for the course You've appointed

You strengthen our hand in every endeavor

In You we shall stand forever and ever

"Sunrise Song"

Totally surrendered
Submitted to His will
Yielded so the Spirit
Will simply come and fill
The quiet of the morning
The birds the only sound
My favorite time to seek Him
When there's no one else around
Solitude surrounds me
I feel supremely blessed
The peace that passes reason
As I enter to His rest
The world the flesh the devil
Have nothing to compare
To the joy and peace I know
When my Saviour comes to share
I humbly thank the Father
As I start another day
For sending forth His Son
So we could have The Way

"Surrender"

Surrender it up
Come fill up your cup
Look past the lies
And find out what's up
Give up control
Let go and let God
Measure your stride
By His staff and His rod
Come down off the throne
And get on your knees
You won't make it alone
But He'll hear your pleas
Surrender is sweet
You don't have to do it
No more control
Let Christ lead you through it
Just pick up your cross
And lay down your life
You shan't suffer loss
What you're losing is strife
Surrender it all
Every day
Answer His call
For He is The Way

"Surrounded"

I feel like I'm surrounded
By people who I love
Still lost in their addictions
Not trusting God above
I see the devil's damage
I feel the hellish chill
It strengthens my conviction
To stay within God's will
I know that I cannot control
The way they think or feel
But hopefully they see in me
That God's grace is for real
My selfish side says flee from these
My spirit bids me stay
I know The One who holds the keys
In Jesus Name I pray
Father I beseech You
Please draw them to that place
Where Your sweet flood of cleansing blood
Will wash them with Your grace
I ask this for my family Lord
From deep within my heart
My faith is great and so I'll wait
And till then do my part

"Teach Me"

Why does it seem so hard Lord
Please teach me how to pray
Give to me a thirst for Thee
Each and every day
I really cannot fathom
Why all it seems I seek
Are things that really don't make sense
And leave me feeling weak
It's crazy how I chase those things
That make me feel so small
All the while neglecting time
With You who made it all
Please help me see distractions
For what they really are
That I may see them coming
And avoid them from afar
I know You are the answer
Please teach me how to ask
That others see You in my face
And not my selfish mask
I ache to be Your servant
Lord help me past my self
Please give me strength to go the length
And leave all that on the shelf
I'm grateful for Your gift of life
The proof that You do care
You've given me so much of it
I've simply got to share

"Tempest"

A storm brings with it wind and rain
As trials bring our lives great pain
The calmness that we knew before
Gets tossed upon life's rocky shore
The scars we get the pain we know
Strengthens us and helps us grow
And while we may not like the feel
These changes are what make us real
And once we've gone through one or two
We learn the best way to get through
Now you can sink or you can swim
But as for me I trust in Him
Regardless of the things you've planned
If it's not His Word on which you stand
A storm will come you will be lost
My friend you can't afford that cost
Come to Christ be safe and warm
He is the shelter from the storm
He will keep you high and dry
But best of all you'll never die
Seek His face and take His hand
He'll take you where the weather's grand

"Testing"

The rapture of my spirit is
The sweetest thing I know
When God tunes out the world around
That to me He may show
His tender love and care for me
It fills me with such joy
As He reminds me when I'm touched
That I am still His boy
At times He overwhelms me with
Such gratitude there's tears
At times His awesome power flows
And shatters all my fears
Sometimes He simply tickles me
And laughter from me bubbles
The times I get to spend with Him
Stay with me through my troubles
From mountain top transfigured
To darkest valley floor
My Jesus is still with me
That's what He came here for
To rescue me to set me free
Deliver me from doom
And though He died they cannot hide
He left an empty tomb
So take heart from those times with Him
Let not your fears deny it
Remember that while testing friend
The Teacher's always quiet

"Tetherball"

The life of a born-again Spirit filled Christian can be likened to that of a game of tetherball. God is the steel pole in the center. It is anchored in concrete it is straight up and does not move. It always stays the same and is the center from which all flows. The rope or "tether" is the Holy Spirit which connects us to God and of course the believer is the ball. The world with all of its trials and tribulations is the fist that strikes or scourges the ball. Every time the fist strikes the ball it drives it on another revolution and as the ball proceeds along its path the tether of the Holy Spirit draws it closer and closer to God in the center. Eventually the ball completes its journey, is at the center, and the game is won. Remember though "Only the ball that gets hit gets moved"

"Thanksgiving"

Father You've taught me to love and to live
For that lesson alone I have thanks to give
You've taught me to care to go forth and give back
You've given me faith that in You there's no lack
The promises which You've engraved on my heart
Have given me rest from Your peace I'll not part
My family my friends and the people I meet
At home and in church and those on the street
Truly a gift to meet them on The Way
A blessing from You to know what to say
My purpose my passion my drive and my health
And O what a gift to have You as my wealth
I may not have money yet still I am rich
The Jennings the Grovers and even Luke Fich
The Whites and the Bishops and the Palmers the same
The Smiths and the rest too many to name
Thanks for Your Word Your sweet bread of life
The sharpest of swords it cuts through all strife
Thank you my Lord for my town and my nation
But first and foremost for Your gift of salvation
Thanks to You Father to Your Son and Your Spirit
You know my heart but You still love to hear it
So I'm just giving back cause You gave me each word
Oh yeah' let's not forget Dad thanks for the bird
(Happy Thanksgiving)

"The Big Swim"

The life and journey of a Christian may be likened to that of the great salmon. We are born into the world and right away we are taught and told to go with the flow, so we get out into the river of life and try to get along. As we flow along with the current we eventually find ourselves out there in the roiling boiling sea of humanity.

There in the chaos and tumult of it all we have an encounter with our Lord and Saviour Jesus Christ. As His sheep we turn and follow the Good Shepherd only now instead of flowing along with the current of the world we must swim against it and fight every inch of the way with little or no rest from the relentless pull of the world going in the other direction.

All along The Way we must learn to avoid baited hooks designed to ensnare us, poisons and toxins which weaken or sicken us, rocks which bruise, batter, and tear our flesh, and seemingly insurmountable dams which halt our progress until we have located the narrow gate of passage that usually consists of a series of steps that we must climb in stages.

Finally after a long and arduous journey full of trials and tribulation constantly being pulled at by the world but at the same time being led by the Holy Spirit back to the Source from Whom everything flows and by Whom all things consist, we find ourselves battered, bruised, torn, and decaying, mere shells or shadows of our former selves physically but infinitely wiser and stronger spiritually and emotionally due to the fact that now in our weakened physical condition we are now relying on Him for all of our strength.

At long last we have completed our course and finished the race. Hopefully as we fall to the ground as that dying seed, where we are sown many more will spring forth into new life.

One last thing, try not to get smoked along the way.

"The Body"

Lord God the Father He is the heart

From whence all the issues of life get their start

No man has seen Him and nobody knows

He is the Source from whom everything flows

Jesus His Son so divine and serene

He is the Face all that we've ever seen

He came down and took on a physical form

Healing and teaching and calming the storm

The Spirit of Truth He is the Voice

Leading us daily to make the right choice

He quickens our spirits and leads us along

Shedding His love and making us strong

We need His strength to meet all demands

For we are His children and we are the Hands

From the Heart to the Face to the Voice and the Hand

Sealed with perfection united we stand

Thank You our Father, Spirit, and Son

For loving us all and making us One

"Fill us Lord"

"The Call"

For God so loved the world
That He gave His only Son
That all men might be saved
Yes each and every one
For God sent not His Son
To condemn the world
But there upon the Cross
Love's Banner was unfurled
But many men won't heed
When they hear the Gospel's call
And that is just so sad
Cause they're headed for a fall
The Father He will draw you
His Son will meet you there
And His Spirit in your heart
Will teach you how to care
So come pick up your cross
And lay your burdens down
To each that overcomes
He's promised them a crown
Come break the Bread of life
Come drink His holy Wine
Come have your sins washed clean
In the Lamb's Blood so divine
(John 3:13-21)

"The Cross"

There I overcame my loss
Upon my knees before the Cross
My Father drew me to that place
Despite my sin to show His grace
He drew me there to set me free
Upon that Cross Christ died for me
And dying there He shed His Blood
And washed me in its cleansing flood
The man I was he died as well
I'm born again and freed from hell
The cross which I now gladly bear
I'm privileged to simply share
Lifted up twixt earth and sky
My Saviour chose that day to die
To make a way for us to win
The spotless Lamb was turned to sin
Of all the pains the one most grim
Was when the Father turned from Him
To make sure I was justified
Upon that Cross my Saviour died
Forsake the world with all its gloss
Come now sinner to the Cross

(1 Corinthians 1:23, Galatians 2:20)

"The Cure"

The sins of the fathers
Affect their children all
And though it may be hard to see
The consequences fall
Not that we meant to harm them
But sin has that effect
It always harms the ones we love
In ways we don't expect
Past actions are related
To circumstances now
When sowing seeds with sinful acts
How bloody cuts the plow
And when then comes the harvest
Though sometimes it takes years
The first fruit of that season
Is always reaped with tears
I can't go back and change things
I cannot change my past
My only course of action now
To do my very best
To be a dad that isn't bad
And just leave God the rest
He will do the healing
Of that I must be sure
For all the pain I've ever caused
'Tis Christ the only Cure

"The Fall"

Once God had made man he needed a place
To dwell with his wife and father a race
So He brought forth a garden with every good tree
He called it Eden where Adam could be
After He made it He proceeded to bless it
Then He put Adam in it to keep it and dress it
He gave Him the trees and the fruit the whole lot
But the fruit of the one in the midst He gave not
He said listen My son for I do not lie
If you eat of it's fruit you will surely die
Then He said it's not good that man is alone
So He caused him to sleep and took his rib bone
Bone of his bones and flesh of his flesh
Now man had a woman they started out fresh
They were both naked the man and his wife
And they knew no shame they simply lived life
This time in the garden this innocent age
Would come to a close as we turn the page
Now the serpent was subtle with a mouth full of guile
Casting doubt on God's Word that is his style
He came at the woman and told her his lie
Said eat of the fruit for ye shall not die
For in the day that you eat it then shall ye see
Knowledge you'll have as a god ye shall be
She looked at the fruit and it did look sweet
So she took a bite and her husband did eat
Then their eyes were opened and they were to blame
They sewed fig leaves together to cover their shame
Then came God's voice in the cool of the day
From the presence of God they both hid away

God called out to Adam where art thou O where
He said I am hiding for my body is bare
Who said you were naked how could this be
Did you eat of the fruit of that only tree
Then Adam said something that truly was flawed
For he blamed his wife and he even blamed God
Then God asked the woman what have you done
She blamed the serpent said he is the one
Then God cursed the serpent and said you can trust
You'll go on your belly and you shall eat dust
And there shall be hatred between yours and her seed
For He'll bruise your head with His heel for this deed
To the woman He said in sorrow and pain
You'll bring forth your seed and your husband shall reign
Then He said to Adam since you chose your wife
I'm cursing this ground ye shall work all your life
Sharp thorns and thistles shall trouble your field
But by the sweat of thy brow bread it will yield
Toil you shall know your whole life through
For dust you came from and dust you'll go to
Then came the first death God took coats of skin
As the first blood was shed to cover their sin
God said to them both now you must go
Of good and of evil now you both know
For My tree of life gives life that's forever
And your access to it I must now sever
So they went forth from Eden away from the Lord
He placed cherubim there with a flaming sharp sword
Way back in the garden man made a bad call
And that is the reason we call it the fall

"The Fool"

There's no God says the fool deep down in his heart
From wisdom and knowledge and light he doth part
They're corrupt and they're wicked and just downright no good
Doing nothing that's holy like a righteous man should
The Lord looked down on them from high up above
To see just how many were seeking His love
But they were all gone aside all together just rotten
None sought after Him they had all just forgotten
They had all become filthy yes they'd all gone aside
They were all filled with hatred lust envy and pride
They feed on the people as if they were bread
They use and abuse them and leave them for dead
There's fear in their bellies deep down in their guts
Cause instead of Yahweh they got the yeah buts
They've shame in their hearts for the weak and the poor
They're simply too busy and they're all keeping score
The house and the job or some dope and a heist
Whatever it is they're too busy for Christ
They can't see Him or hear Him or touch taste or smell
It's really too bad cause they'll end up in hell
If they'd just simply ask for some spiritual eyes
But they're just too caught up in Beelzebub's lies
When I think of their fate my heart it doth yearn
We must show them the Way before all of them burn
Thank You Lord Jesus for the hunger and thirst
To spread forth Your Gospel and put others first
(Psalm 14)

"The Four Horsemen"

When John saw the Lamb break the first seal
The voice of a beast like thunder did peal
Come and see he did say so John looked around
Behold a white horse and a rider that's crowned
With a crown on his head and a bow in his hand
He rides forth in battle to conquer the land
The next seal was broken and there came a red horse
And he that sat on it was given great force
To rob earth of peace and turn brother on brother
By the great sword he bears they shall kill one another
The third seal was cracked the next horse was black
And he that sat on him would bring a great lack
With balance in hand to measure and weigh
Starvation and famine will rule in that day
The next seal was opened and this horse was pale
And what he brings with him will make the world wail
For he who sits on him robs men of their breath
He brings hell on earth for his name it is death
These are the four horsemen and they are for real
They shall mount up and ride when the Lamb breaks the seal

"The Gift"

It's quiet here on Christmas morn
On this tier where hearts are torn
This is a very special day
Our families are so far away
The kids around the Christmas tree
The gift they miss is seeing me
Of all the foolish things I've done
Not being there is the worst one
I miss my kids I miss my wife
The things I did screwed up my life
Of all the things that I have missed
The smiles, the hugs, the kiss un-kissed
The one that is the most unfair
Is that they think I just don't care
I've broke their hearts and stole their joy
That can't be fixed with a card or toy
It takes a lot to be a Dad
There is no room for being bad
The things in life that serve your self
Must not be taken off the shelf
Hate and pride and lust and greed
Are not the things our families need
But time attention care and love

Someone to point them up above
These are the things a man must do
To grow a family strong and true
After all these years behind these bars
All the tears and all the scars
My ears can hear my eyes can see
I have no fear I've been set free
Lord the greatest Gift You ever gave
The Son You sent to seek and save
He lived and died and made a way
For us to follow Him and stay
Forever in Your loving arms
Safe from danger and all harms
Yes for all of us His flesh was torn
It's quiet here on Christmas morn

Thank You Lord
Christmas Day 2008

"The Godly Man"

As light flows down from outer space
And beats upon my upturned face
It dawns on me what I can be
Now that Christ has set me free
Within my heart His plans unfold
And though I age I feel not old
Each new day feels fresh and clean
He shows me things I've never seen
The beauty that I now can see
Was always here surrounding me
It's crazy how things focused in
Once I chose to turn from sin
All those years of useless doubt
I now know Christ will work it out
For even when I feel great pain
I learn from that and so there's gain
For toil and snare and wicked plan
Mean nothing to the godly man

"The Good Shepherd"

Verily, verily, I say unto thee
He that sneaks in wicked is he
He's not the Shepherd he comes to steal
The sheep know the Shepherd His voice is real
They follow Him for He keeps them from danger
He calls them by name but they flee from the stranger
Verily, verily, I say unto you
He is the Door what I tell you is true
All of the others liars were they
They weren't the Life the Truth or the Way
He is the door all must go through
If you enter not there is no hope for you
The thief comes to steal to kill and destroy
While He comes to bring life that you might enjoy
He is the Good Shepherd He lays down His life
He'll lead, feed, preserve you, keep you through strife
He gives His life freely out of pure love
Which He gets from the Father high up above
His sheep aren't alone He has many others
They must understand that all men are brothers
His sheep hear His voice and they follow Him
There's no need to sink for He'll teach them to swim
He gives to His sheep a life that's forever
Secure in His hand which no man can sever
Yes no man is able to take from the Son
What He got from the Father for they are both One
(John Chapter 10)

"The Gospel"

Forsworn forlorn a receiver of scorn
A man of sorrows our Redeemer was torn
To answer for our sin and pride
Christ came down and bled and died
The things He did the things He said
Mean so much more for He's not dead
And though they laid Him in that grave
From death's dark grip He'd also save
For Friday's dark and bloody gloom
Does not compare with Sunday's bloom
Our Saviour lives He rose that day
He had more things to do and say
And when He'd made His presence known
Ascending up He took His throne
The brothers watched Him tread the sky
And there He's seated up on high
To help us cope and find our way
He sent His Spirit down to stay
Here He dwells in each one's heart
He strengthens us to do our part
And so our hope would have no lack
He's promised us He's coming back!!!

"The Length of His Strength"

The glory of God the heavens declare
The firmament showeth His hand everywhere
Day after day uttereth speech
The stars in the night too high too reach
No language or speech voice or known tongue
Leave's God's awesome glory in creation unsung
Throughout all the earth and the entire world
His majesty reigns supremely unfurled
In them He's set up a house for the sun
As a bridegroom coming with a race to be run
His route spans the heavens clear out to the ends
And nothing is hid from the heat that He sends
The Lord's laws are perfect converting the soul
His Gospel is pure to make the wise whole
There's joy in my heart for His statutes are right
His commandments are sure and they give my eyes light
The fear of the Lord is clean and forever
His judgments are sure in every endeavor
They're finer than gold and sweeter than honey
They never grow old and they're better than money
By them Thy servant is afforded right warning
And he who keeps them is rewarded by morning
Who can tell why his heart it doth error
Cleanse me inside keep me from terror
Keep me back Lord from the sins of the heart
With Your Holy Word let every day start
Let not the foul pride of life have its way
Come fill me inside and lead me each day
Let the words of my mouth and my hearts meditations
Be worthy of You in all situations
You paid a great price you went the whole length
You are my Redeemer and You are my Strength
(Psalm 19)

"The Light"

God gave us a gift to show us the way
It brings to us warmth and brightens the day
It shines in the darkness it's warm and it's bright
The gift that I speak of is what we call light
It flows from it's Source right out through space
To feed every plant and warm every face
It gives us the colors we see in the sky
And by it we measure the days that go by
But there is a light that cannot be seen
It can only be known if you know what I mean
This light comes from wisdom that's where it doth start
Etched by God's hand deep down in your heart
Yes there is a dawn that starts out each day
And one in your mind when you see the way
We all know the sun that hangs in the sky
But who knows the One who came here to die
The light from the one brightens the day
While God's only Son shows us the Way
He came here for all yes He's yours and He's mine
If you have His light Brother let that light shine!!!!

"The Lord's Prayer"

Corporate Intercession
Join hands and let us pray
As God above looks down with love
And hears that which we say
Let honor praise and glory
Precede His Holy Name
Let heartfelt adoration
Be expressed to Him the same
Let His will be requested
From each and every heart
Give each the strength to go the length
And from His Way not part
Next let us ask provision
Please give us daily bread
Not only for our bodies
But by His Word be fed
Now let us ask forgiveness
For that which we have done
And knowing we're forgiven
Have grace for everyone
Let not our hearts be tempted
Instead filled with His light
That we may see and all agree
To do that which is right
Let evil be confounded
Relieve us of that pain
May the power and the glory
Of His Kingdom ever reign

"The Master's Touch"

That pure and gentle Spirit
That covers me at night
Also walks and talks with me
As well in broad daylight
But I can get distracted
When I am wide awake
Yet still my Saviour has my back
Through every last mistake
But when I'm not distracted
And when I get it right
My heart is filled to bursting
With love and joy and light
I see His hand in everything
As with His fingerprints
He reaffirms my faith each day
With subtle little hints
The daily revelations
To me they mean so much
A blessing just to recognize
The Master's gentle touch

"The New"

If any man be found in Christ
Old things are passed away
Behold all things are now made new
The Potter forms the clay
And all things are of God who has
Reconciled us all
And given us a ministry
To go and sound the call
That God Himself became a man
And walked this common ground
That each of us who trusts in Him
Would in Him now be found
And by His holy precious blood
Each one of us is healed
Until redemption's day is dawned
By Blood and Spirit sealed
So take heart and be confident
That work He has begun
He will perform until that day
He sends again His Son
One last thing I must point out
That He told me to tell
He maketh no mistake in you
Our God does all things well
(2 Cor. 5:17, Phil 1:6)

"The One"

As I sit within this cell
Reflecting on my life
I feel like I'm in hell
Damn I miss my wife
The past seems like a nightmare
The present's quite a drag
Though speaking of my future
I feel I have to brag
Now I have been a bastard
At times I've been quite sick
My woman has stood by me
Now that's one solid chick
She makes my life worth living
Of this I must confess
Without the love she's giving
My life would be a mess
I swore that I would love her
That I would always cherish
I know that if I lost her
That I would surely perish
She carries now within her
Our daughter or our son
I praise the Lord for blessing me
And sending me The One

"The Preacher"

Vanity of vanities a vapor or a breath
With nothing we're brought forth
And with nothing we meet death
What does it profit one
To work and slave and toil
Or live one's life for fun
And burn the midnight oil
Pleasures they are fleeting
Worries tear you down
And though a king has riches
He cannot keep his crown
For all things have their season
A time to live and die
No man can find the reason
For only God knows why
The sinner seems to flourish
While the righteous they see strife
But trials they will nourish
And edify your life
To walk beside a brother
Much better than alone
For we can help each other
And so God's love is shown
So what's the whole conclusion
The sum of all we've heard
Don't live in an illusion
And heed God's every Word!

"The Roman Road"

Listen my friends to what I will say
For this is a map to show you the way
Yes pay close attention to what I will tell
For this is the exit from the highway to hell
For broad is the gate and wide is the way
If you stay on that road there'll be hell to pay
The way to get off is narrow and hard
The whole world will laugh and call you retard
But if you stay on this path day after day
Through trial and error you will find your way
These things that I tell you are right and they're true
Believe on His Name and You'll know they are too
To get yourself started and be a beginner
You must first understand that you are a sinner
But not only you for all men fall short
Of the glory of God His Word does report
For one man did sin it's known as the fall
When Adam screwed up it affected us all
The wages of sin is nothing but death
But thanks be to God for the gift of His Breath
For He breathed new life back into our lives
Through the death of His Son on the cross we survive
He did it for love not because we were winners
For He laid down His life while we were yet sinners
Yes the life that He had He freely gave
If you call on His Name then you He will save
This road may get rough like when Paul was in Rome
It may cost you your life but then you'll be home

"The Shepherd's Song"

The Lord is my Shepherd He takes great care
No matter what He's always there
I have no needs unknown to Him
Beneath His wing my life and limb
In fields of green He gives me rest
His bread of life I do ingest
The water that He leads me to
Is still and deep and pure and true
He heals my soul and sets me free
He makes me whole so I can see
He leads me on the path of right
For His Name's sake to shine His light
Yea though I tread through death's dark door
I'll have no fear forever more
Your rod and staff they comfort me
And on this path with You I'm free
The table You've set has my foes disappointed
My cup runneth over my head You've anointed
Surely goodness and mercy all my life shall I see
And the house of the Lord is where forever I'll be

(Psalm 23)

"The Sweetest Peace"

Overwhelming gratitude
For everything You do
For every gift You've blessed me with
And all You've brought me through
Your personal protection when
I lay me down to sleep
Your blessing of assurance
That my soul is Yours to keep
Your strength that keeps me standing
While Your Spirit keeps me meek
Knowing that I know I'm Yours
When things seem very bleak
And even when my body fails
A victim of the curse
Your gentle voice reminds me still
That things could be much worse
The blessing of Your lessons
Shine right through adversity
The gift of Your discernment
What You would have me see
I'm hoping that my focus stays
Firmly fixed on You
Not dwelling on my problems
Or what I'm going through
I know that my persona
Needs not me but Your increase
And laying down my ego
Grants my soul the sweetest peace

"The Tongue"

Remember this my brothers
That if you're called to lead
A higher standard's set for you
For every word and deed
For if you find a bridle
And discipline your tongue
Offense is just not taken and
A holy song is sung
For our tongues can spew poison
The Word says no man tames
That little tongue can spark a war
A forest fire of flames
We praise God with it sometimes
Yet then we curse our fellows
As Satan laughing carries on
Pumping on his bellows
But let the wise man follow
Christ in all His meekness
Even though the world looks on
And mocks our stance as weakness
Since wisdom flows from heaven
It's clear that they don't see
So show them His reflection
That His love may set them free

(James 3:1-18)

"The Vine"

Lord You are the Vine from which we flow

We branch out from You that's how we grow

Lift up our leaves from out of the dust

You feed us with light in You do we trust

Prune us and shear us and take every shoot

Which saps us and drains us and robs us of fruit

Yes cut back the things in our lives that are wrong

That we may endure all the while growing strong

The fruit that we bear comes from deep down inside

We know that You care so in You we abide

"The Way"

Father You've told me that blessed is he

Who forsakes the devil and uses Your key

He delights in Thy precepts he learns them right well

They sharpen his focus and keep him from hell

He meditates in them all day and all night

In them he's learning to walk in the light

His roots growing strong like a tree by the river

In his heart is the song penned by You the life Giver

He never has doubt for You are his reason

All his labour bears fruit from You in due season

The ungodly aren't so for they're gone with the wind

While the righteous shall stand as if they'd never sinned

You've cleared us a path

Through Your Son whom we cherish

Without Him the wicked will all surely perish

Yes Father You've written that blessed is he

Who gladly accepts what You've offered for free

(Psalm 1)

"The Word"

Light in the Old and Love in the New
Testament One and Testament Two
Light for our head and Love for our heart
Where the finish is told as well as the start
The Old One is full of Messiah concealed
The New One is where God's Love is revealed
His Love is poured out in the form of a Man
To reach us and teach us yes that was His plan
He walked and He talked and He bled and He died
Then God raised Him up now He sits at His side
The world's ways are broken the time's drawing near
When the trumpet shall sound for all men to hear
My hope and my prayer is that I will not die
But rise in the air to meet Christ in the sky
Yes I seek His face so I continue to look
Not just in the sky but throughout His whole Book
Deeper and deeper and farther I go
What I learn from its pages helps me to grow
His Spirit it sharpens my innermost sight
He leads me in truth to digest His Bread right
Thank You my Father for the hunger and thirst
To learn Your Word better chapter and verse
Not just what it says but what is the meaning
And to put into use all the truth I am gleaning
To walk Your Word out and live it for true
To shine forth Your light and lead others to You

(Proverbs 30:5,6)

"Thirst"

Born aloft by majesty buoyed by Your love
Your Spirit fills my heart to burst stretched out just like a glove
I can't describe the feeling though Lord You know I've tried
When thinking of the mess I'd made for which my Saviour died
Amidst the pain and chaos You came and sought me there
Even in my darkest hour You had me in Your care
Your hand of grace upon me no matter what I did
For even though I knew it not I was still Your kid
Then one day like a light switch You opened up my eyes
To recognize the mess I'd made a tangled web of lies
Half-truths and philosophies wrong thoughts which kept me sick
You cut right through confusion with just one simple click
So now I have my lights on and I can finally see
The truest freedom I can know comes from serving Thee
I pray for daily guidance to clearly hear Your voice
And automatic hunger to make the proper choice
No matter what You're with me of that I have no doubt
And even when I make mistakes I know You'll work it out
Another twenty-four Lord yes another day to stand
And do just what You'd have me to Your will my heart's command
I pray for wisdom strength and love compassion in my heart
And for the thirst to put You first and always do my part

"Three and One"

The Father Son and Holy Ghost

Are the Ones I love the most

The Love and Grace which they bestow

Restore my soul and make me grow

The Father leads me every day

Directs my steps along the way

And late at night while I'm asleep

The Son stands guard my soul to keep

And when I wake and meet the day

His Spirit comes with things to say

The things He tells me still my heart

He gives me strength each day to start

No matter what a day may bring

It's still His Song I choose to sing

I give my life to serve His throne

And that my friend is etched in Stone

(Proverbs 6:22)

"Throne Room"

I cannot say exactly when
But soon will come my day and then
They will tell me I am free
And there's no place I'd rather be
Than on my face before Your throne
Where I can make my wishes known
And You can tell me what I need
To be effective planting seed
Where You'll reveal to me Your will
While I am yielded quiet and still
But really I can do that now
Gradually I'm learning how
To free myself of worldly things
And feel the peace Your presence brings
For fences bricks and walls of stone
Dissolve when I'm before Your throne
When there I learn what's right and true
A blessing just to speak with You
Thank You Father for the space
That surrounds Your throne of grace

(Hebrews 4:16)

"Time"

There is a thing that simply won't last
It flows from our future into our past
You can't see hear or touch it and it has no taste
And it's really a shame when it is a waste
We have one to be born and one to die
It waits for no man it simply goes by
Some call it father and some say it's slippin
Some it won't faze while some folks are trippin
We are told to redeem it for life's not a game
But most of us won't and that's just a shame
We keep it and share it and spend it and take it
But one thing we can't do is simply to make it
Some try to kill it some have lots to do
While many are blind and have not a clue
It wears out our flesh and breaks us all down
It can turn a young smile to an old frown
We each have so much and that's all we get
And there's only one way to live beyond it
Yours it is coming and mine it is too
We each need to decide what we're going to do
The truth of it is there's none left to lose
Its end's drawing near so hurry and choose
Deep down inside there is a small voice
Asking us all what will be your choice
Have you figured out the source of this rhyme
My brothers and sisters I'm speaking of time
(Ephesians 5:14-16)

"Today"

Where are you going what do you do

Can't you hear God calling to you

Come to the Cross to the Lamb that was slain

Bring Him your sorrows your worries your pain

Lay down your burdens and pick up your cross

The things of this world count all that as loss

Let your heart break let tears wash your face

As He cleanses your soul with mercy and grace

Boldly He tells us to come to His throne

That His awesome love may be fully known

He knocks in your heart don't send Him away

Tomorrow's not promised **Today is the Day!**

(2 Corinthians 6:2)

"Together"

Time has a way of slipping by
No man can say just how or why
But things will come and they will go
The way things change is how we grow
You cannot hold on to the past
Those things were never meant to last
And while tomorrow will come round
We need our balance and our ground
Today is where we need our sight
To seize the day and live it right
So focus on the here and now
Keep your hands upon the plow
One step two step three step four
That's what He gave us two feet for
So if it's nice or stormy weather
Friend just keep yourself together
Don't be anxious don't get spun
And set your compass to the Son

(Matthew 6:33,34)

"Torches"

Lately we have been quite blessed
Our Brother Joe has been our guest
He comes here as our Saviour's ARM
With goodly cheer and godly charm
I'm confident and have high hopes
That he will help me learn the ropes
For where he is I long to be
Helping set the captives free
He's showing me a brand new way
To power pack a real short stay
I love the way he calls me Brother
We are meant to know each other
And let me not forget this part
Thank You Lord for Brother Art
I feel truly greatly blessed
I'm learning from the very best
I know these brothers truly care
They'll bear their torches anywhere
Thank You Father for these ones
An honor just to know Your sons
One last prayer I do confide
That I may serve You by their side

"Tossed"

Double minded my dilemma distracted to be sure

Pressing in the only absolutely efficacious cure

Even though I know this and I have not one slim doubt

My mind still wants to wander and so I thrash about

Like a ship tossed on the ocean crashing on the waves

I simply must remember that only Jesus saves

Not only from perdition nor from the lake of flames

But also from the madness of this world's senseless games

Peaceful calm contentedness is there for me to claim

I know that all I have to do is call upon His Name

And when delighted in Him I simply have to say

All my selfish wants and lusts they simply fade away

Still longing for the day when my loneliness is done

And so my daily prayer is that He will send the one

The one who will walk with me and always have my back

One whom I may care for that she may know no lack

Yes loneliness my thorn Lord please take it now from me

Give to me that single eye that sees nothing Lord but Thee

For now I'll just quit whining and be grateful for Your care

Despite my loneliness remember You are always there

Prince of Peace becalm the waters please bid them now be still

That I may enter to Your rest and simply do Your will

"Trials"

Trials come and trials go
Through trials we are sure to grow
They toughen us and make us strong
No matter what they still seem wrong
Without the wind a tree falls down
But with it roots will hold the ground
Now rain will come and it will fall
Without it things won't grow at all
But in the midst of tribulations
We can handle situations
We can win or we can lose
It's up to us we have to choose
And though things may seem quite unfair
If you take them to the Lord in prayer
He will lead you as you walk
And plant you firmly on His Rock
So before you run or lose your cool
And act just like some silly fool
Consider what you've read and heard
From God's eternal written Word
Within it are the keys to life
To carry you through every strife
One more thing before you're through
Please thank the Lord for testing you

"Tune In"

From a thunderbolt's crack to the sigh of the wind

Or the cry in your heart when you know you have sinned

From the whine of a skeeter to the buzz of a bee

Or the breath of your lover that sets your heart free

From the boiling white waves that crash on the shore

To the gentle sweet knocking on your hearts inner door

From the birds sweetly singing and greeting the morn

To the sad sound of weeping when someone is torn

From the laughter of children as they play in the yard

To the pounding of blood from running real hard

From the sound of a hymn when you're singing it out

To the sound of the Gospel when it's preached with no doubt

All of these things yes every last one

Are notes in the Song that sing of the Son

For He is the reason this world goes around

And He is the Author of every last sound

So tune your receiver sharpen your sword

Just be a believer and trust in the Lord

"Ubiquitous"

Whilst I lay me down to sleep or rising in the morn
Standing tall in victory or broken small and torn
It matters not where I may find my circumstances lay
You are right there with me Lord each and every day
In each and every moment each heartbeat and each breath
Deep within my mother's womb yes even after death
No matter where my soul may roam no matter where I go
There is no height nor dark abyss You don't already know
Upon the raging ocean storm or coolest blue lagoon
The burning surface of the sun the dark side of the moon
The joy that fills my laughter the pain that salts my tears
You give me faith to carry on despite my darkest fears
I cannot live without You my soul knows that right well
Though seated in the heavenlies
You've carried me through hell
And even at my very worst You gave not up on me
You've shed Your precious Holy Blood just to set me free
My words don't do You justice yet still my pen must write
For through the gift of poetry Your Holy Spirit might
And so I will continue to frame my prose with care
As I take heart to do my part as You are always there

"Unending Love"

Firmly focused on ourselves
Every single day
Fill us with Your Spirit Lord
Teach us how to pray
Let our hearts be broken for
Those people that we see
Who do not know Your peace at all
Who have not trusted Thee
Give to us a heart that's Yours
Which overflows with grace
Even for the ones who mock
Or wear an angry face
Teach us to be patient Lord
Not always in a hurry
Increase the measure of our faith
That we may never worry
Let us focus on Your things
Not merely on our own
Give to us a heart that longs
To kneel before Your throne
Cure us of our endless quest
For glass and chrome and steel
Fill our hearts with Your desires
For all that stands as real
Yes let our minds be focused on
Those things which are above
Let Heaven now invade our hearts
With Your unending Love

"Unite"

In the twilight's last gleaming

I can still see a spark

Of the fire that burns

And beats back the dark

Like a city that shines

Atop a great hill

The freedom to speak

Abides with us still

We may not be perfect

And we've gotten off track

But it's still not too late

We can still make it back

The land of the free

And the home of the brave

Needs to focus on God

Not the blessings He gave

We need to unite

And again stand as one

A nation committed

To serving the Son

"Untitled"

The vacant place the empty little cot

We see them day by day

And oh, it fills our hearts with care

Since our loved one went away

But though the light has left us here

Like the setting of the sun

We'll trust Thee ever, Father dear

And say "Thy will be done"

Grace Hayes

"A Valentine"

As Valentine's is drawing near

Remember that I love you dear

And though we are so far apart

We live within each other's heart

The little things you say and do

Stick in my mind like super glue

To hear your voice or see your smile

I'd gladly crawl a country mile

The thing I think I miss the most

To snuggle up and hold you close

I know this is just a silly poem

And you would rather have me home

But honey don't you have one doubt

I promise you when I get out

I'll take you out to wine and dine

Then I will be your Valentine

"Valiant"

You do not call the qualified You qualify the called
And when You call me in to serve let my heart be enthralled
I humbly ask for wisdom Lord when reaching forth my hand
Please bless all I put it to and give me strength to stand
I need not know Your purpose Lord in everything You do
Just let me be obedient and strong and right and true
And when I face new challenges let not my heart be troubled
But in those times increase my faith my portion of it doubled
Please let my mine eye be single Lord so firmly fixed on You
That Your will is my first concern in everything I do
And as the soaring eagle knows when lifted up in flight
'Tis not his strength that carries him he's lofted by Your might
Let not my fears control me diminishing my walk
But let me speak Your Truth in love calm boldness when I talk
I pray Your still meek power would radiate from me
Your blessed calm assurance that comes from being free
And when I'm persecuted mocked or scorned or beat
Give me strength and courage to never know defeat
Please keep me ever conscious that all I'm going through
Is merely meant to strengthen me conforming me to You
One last thing I pray for if it is not too much
Let all I put my hands to receive Your master touch
I know You always hear me Lord so let me always pray
That I may walk in victory each and every day

"Victim's Awareness"

Indulging in my nature I've made things quite a mess
Of this I have not one slim doubt and so I do confess
I've slandered and made mockery of all that's right and true
And worse than that I've led astray convincing others too
Concocting my own doctrine passed off as brotherhood
Misguided misconceptions unrighteous seeming good
Finding and devising ways to make my sin seem cool
Convincing others I was wise when I was but a fool
Putting so much energy into the wrong direction
Convinced that I was righteous as I spread my own infection
The fruits of all these labors bore an essence of their own
Loneliness and prison sets for all the seeds I'd sown
A bitter hollow harvest hard enough for me to bear
Yet precious hearts were hardened thinking that I did not care
Convinced my sins were mine alone deserving privacy
But sin affects us one and all that's been revealed to me
One cannot simply harm one's self you're always harming others
For what we do unto ourselves we do unto our brothers
So next time that you contemplate a little private sin
Consider the unwilling victims you are dragging in

"Victory"

To live without a purpose
Is not to live at all
To fly so high you touch the sky
The prelude to a fall
Practically forgotten
The stupid things I did
To run and gun and live for fun
When I was just a kid
But now as life continues
Those things have run their course
Think change not strange it's prearranged
As growth flows from The Source
For nothing will continue
To stay as it has been
Through God's redeeming power
I'm growing out of sin
I've learned that self reliance
Eventually just drags
For even at my finest
I'm dressed in filthy rags
I celebrate each victory
No credit to me due
For every battle I have won
Twas Christ that brought me through

"Wait"

Surrendered I am in Your hands
Your way is best I trust Your plans
And though things might not yet be clear
I have no doubts I have no fear
Cause even when I've done my best
To mess things up I've still been blessed
Yes even when I left Your will
You brought me back and loved me still
But that was then I'm different now
I'll wait for You to show me how
The patience that You're teaching me
Is clearly meant for me to see
A better way to live and love
And seek those things which are above
Where moth and rust doth not destroy
And all my tears are turned to joy
Thank You Lord for seeing me through
And for teaching me how to wait on You

(Isaiah 40:31)

"Wake Up America"

I will praise Thee O Lord with all of my heart
I'll show forth Your works that's where I will start
I'll be glad and rejoice and sing praise to Thy Name
Most High El Shaddai of Israel's fame
When my enemies come they are quickly turned back
They fall and they perish it's Your Spirit they lack
For Thou hast maintained my right and my cause
I walk in Thy ways and I delight in Thy laws
You've rebuked the heathen and the wicked destroyed
At times Your death angel You've even employed
My foes are cast down and swift was their end
How final and just the judgment You send
Forever and ever You shall endure
Your wisdom is holy Your righteousness pure
Lord You are a refuge for all the oppressed
In trials and perils with safety they're blessed
He avenges them all remembers the humble
He makes smooth their path so they will not stumble
Have mercy on me consider my trouble
All those who hate me make their portion double
The heathen fall down in the pit they have made
They've dug their own grave how low they are laid
The wicked shall turn straight into hell
And all of the nations that forget God as well
So let's turn around before it's too late
We all know that God made this country great
Let's turn from our sins before we're undone
God give us the courage to follow Your Son
(Psalm 9)

"What We Won't See"

No pain no death no fear no loss

No guilt no shame no bloodstained cross

No hate no scorn no war no strife

No more disease no end to life

No more wickedness and sin

No more fears that we won't win

No more struggle no more strain

No more cobwebs in the brain

No more darkness no more grief

No more doubt nor disbelief

No more hurry no more crime

No more worry no more time

These are some things that we won't see

When Jesus comes and sets us free

"What's the Point"

Cast about by doctrines
From wave to crashing wave
The double minded man becomes
His intellects own slave
He'll often quote with confidence
Those random things he's heard
Instead of testing them against
God's unchanging Word
Like grass that withers in the sun
Or vapors that dissolve
His never ceasing racing mind
Will never ever solve
The riddle of the mystery
That haunts his waking dreams
Unfulfilled conquistador
Is nothing what it seems?
Perhaps he's pouring out his life
Towards altruistic goals
How wicked is the "good" that won't
Warn men about their souls
I say all this so you don't miss
This point I make to you
When men look on you with respect
Who do you point them to?

"Where's Your Trust?"

Cursed is he that trusteth in man
His flesh is his strength and he has his own plan
His heart has departed he's forsaken the Lord
He takes what he wants and he lives by the sword
Like a shrub in the desert he sees not what's good
He's dry and he's brittle like old rotten wood
But he who trusts God blessed is he
He's tall and he's strong with roots like a tree
He always bears fruit and his leaves they are green
He fears not the drought and in heat he's serene
The heart is deceitful and wicked and dark
But the Lord counts the rings right through the bark
He searches the heart He tries the reins
To give every man what he's earned for his pains
From takers He'll take all that they've stored
While givers receive an eternal reward
A curse or a blessing it's all up to you
So make up your mind and do what you do
(Jeremiah 17:5-10)

"Whisper"

Dig a trench about this altar
And drench it with your doubt
Mockery and scorn
Won't put God's fire out
Jump and shout and scream
And carry on my friend
It's all just so much steam
Makes no difference in the end
You have a thousand answers
And endless reasons why
You won't accept the Truth
You're strung out on the lie
But as for me I'm standing
On the promise that God made
When He sent His only Son
And my debt to hell was paid
I hope you find your bottom
And there you make the choice
To see past Satan's lies
And listen to God's voice
Patiently He's calling
He wants you to be free
His whisper in your heart
Says "Come now follow Me"
(Matthew 11:28-30)

"Whoooooh"

Ruach, Pnuema, Spirit, Breath

Quicken me wake me from death

Stir me deep within my soul

Bind up the breach and make me whole

Heal the wound from Satan's stroke

Let Your beam cut through the smoke

I was brought forth already torn

But now in You I am reborn

Born once die twice that is the deal

Born twice die once the Spirit's seal

I once was blind but now I see

Since You've blown Your breath on me

Ja Schu Ha in the Sky

All I know Yahweh high

Thank You Lord for grafting me

To Your eternal family tree

"Willingness"

Willingness is as willingness does
Not what you will but what is because
The things that we would are not what we do
But what we get done that is what's true
Willing to what willing to give
Willing to serve willing to live
Willing to share willing to care
Willing to love and always be there
Are you willing to change to learn and to grow
To look deep inside and tell yourself no
Don't tell me you'll try for that is a lie
A pre-fabbed excuse just as to why
You've failed again cause you couldn't do it
Don't lie to yourself just get up and get to it
Willingness says enough is enough
The truth of it is it's not really that tough
Just go to the Lord for power He brings
Through Him you will see that you can do all things
(Philippians 4:13,19)

"Windshield Full of Woes"

Way back in the Garden of Eden when Adam sinned, it was a lot like when you are driving down the road and a rock chips your windshield. It might not seem like much at the time but through the wear and tear of time and the vibrations from the road, that little chip turns into a crack that grows with each passing day. Every bump in the road, every drop of rain or piece of hail, endless hot days with the sun just beating down on it heating it up, every time you slam the door or the hood, not to mention the constant vibration from the motor. All of these forces contribute to the size of that crack and weakens the whole windshield. You see it and you just know its days are numbered and that soon the whole thing must be completely taken out and replaced with a brand new one, this is the sad condition of our broken, sin-cursed world, and try as he might, man with his mortal man-made solutions will never ever be able to fix it. Only the Lord God in His infinite wisdom has a perfect seamless plan. His supernatural solution supersedes countless silly attempts to fix this broken world, He is the Potter and this world is His to re-shape into a flawless vessel when it pleases Him to do so. Only His mercy and longsuffering patience have allowed it to continue this long.

"Maranatha"

"Wisdom"

The wisest man to ever live
Left behind what he could give
The blessing that he got in Kings
Throughout his Proverbs truly rings
Of justice judgment equity
The wise will learn and be set free
To fear the Lord is where they start
But fools despise and soon depart
Wisdom's voice is loud and clear
But fools are just too proud to hear
They laugh and scorn and mock her voice
But they will soon regret their choice
While those who hearken unto her
Shall safely dwell their way is sure
If thou wilt her words receive
And in your heart you do believe
Yes if thou wilt incline thine ear
Your heart shall be washed free of fear
And if it brings you joy and pleasure
To seek her as a precious treasure
The Lord will come and take your hand
So that you may understand
By her the Lord did found the earth

And gave the heavens all their birth
In her right hand is length of days
And pleasantness marks all her ways
A tree of life to them is she
To them who grasp her golden key
A crown of glory she shall give
With grace she'll teach you how to live
So take fast hold of her instruction
And she will keep you from destruction
Beware of what the world calls wise
It's based on Satan's foolish lies
Prosperity and much success
Can leave one' life a total mess
So get your wisdom from the Lord
And sharpen up your spirit's sword
Yes Solomon did finally say
Fear God my son and just obey

"Witness"

The dogs of war are at your door
They have an axe to grind
For if you don't bow down with them
They're sworn to kill your kind
Grace is not their program
Their book speaks naught of love
Yet they insist all must do this
A mandate from above
They have so many allies
They're known by many names
Power is their drug of choice
And wicked are their games
They steal connive and simply thrive
They seem to run it all
But I can tell you this my friend
They're headed for a fall
Things aren't getting any better
They're only getting worse
I see the signs and note the times
I learned them verse by verse
Yes long ago this was foretold
So take note and move on
Don't get caught up in madness now
Don't be the devil's pawn
Instead look to our Saviour
His example left for you
O' Father please forgive them
For they know not what they do

"Working Man"

A working man's honest

A working man's true

A working man knows the things he must do

He rises up to meet the day

And earns his keep for honest pay

He works with his hands

That he may help others

And so he commands the respect of his brothers

He shows up on time he does what is needed

And the job is not done till the task is completed

A working man's strong

A working man's tough

A working man knows when enough is enough

And after a week of doing his best

The working man takes a much needed rest

"Yoked"

The path of least resistance
When herded by one's fears
Seems to be the safest bet
But only ends in tears
Broad and wide you'll safely slide
Smoothly through that gate
It seems so nice but what a price
Once you see that it's too late
No pain no gain it's very plain
For every eye to see
That nothing that's worth having
Ever comes for free
Eternity began for you
Within your mother's womb
You need to get it figured out
Before you reach your tomb
That narrow rocky uphill climb
Against the current's flow
Will only make you stronger
And cause your heart to grow
Stronger with each step of faith
Your eyes begin to see
The bondage and the shackles
The world calls being free
A pipe dream of deception
Just shiny mirrors and smoke
The path to yield a harvest
Takes sweat and plow and yoke

"You"

Delivered by Your mercy through Your boundless grace
Only when I turn from You can I not see Your face
You're always right before me no matter where I go
In all I see You're training me so I will always know
You raised majestic mountains You poured the raging seas
You put each roadblock in my path and brought me to my knees
Your patience is astounding for this I know right well
For forty years I caused You tears speeding right towards hell
And still You never gave me up no matter what I did
A prodigal there is no doubt confused but still Your kid
Today my life's so different chaos no longer rules
For in Your Word You've given me a perfect set of tools
Tools to set my course by and tools to understand
All that lies before me fashioned by Your sovereign hand
At times You leave me speechless at times I have to pause
Reflecting on Your mercy despite my many flaws
I want to thank You Father I want to spend my days
Learning more about You and Your gentle ways
Your judgement is so perfect so right so strong so true
And gratitude my attitude when I think of You
Please keep me near Your heart Lord let Your Spirit flow
And let me shine Your light so bright that others too may know
Defying all description how many things You do
I really want to thank You Lord for simply being You

"Your Word"

Deep down in my heart
I've hid Thy Word within
Holding to the hope
Against Thee I won't sin
The way of truth I choose
Please put me not to shame
And always give me strength
To glorify Your Name
A light unto my path
A lamp unto my feet
Like honey to my tongue
Your Word is oh so sweet
With trembling flesh I seek
To only know Your will
Emptied of my self
A vessel You would fill
There's nothing I have seen
Or thought or read or heard
That even holds a candle to
Your precious Holy Word
(Psalm 119)

To schedule a testimony, selected reading, or book signing please contact James directly at the following email address. Comments and feedback always welcome.

ironsaints1@gmail.com

May the peace of Christ dwell in you richly and thank you for your support!

Made in the USA
Lexington, KY
09 February 2017